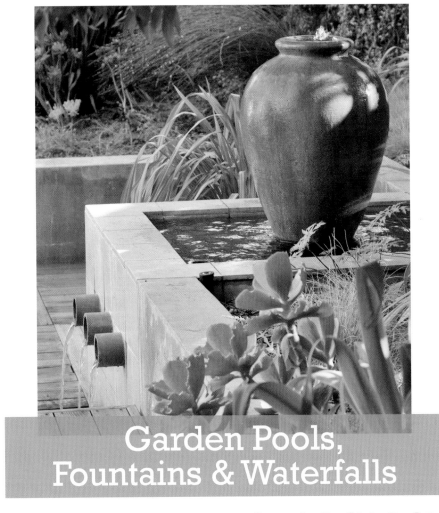

Garden Pools, Fountains & Waterfalls

A *Sunset* Outdoor Design & Build Guide

By Debra Prinzing and the Editors of *Sunset*

Sunset

©2012 by Time Home Entertainment Inc.
135 West 50th Street, New York, NY 10020

ISBN-13: 978-0-376-01430-6   ISBN-10: 0-376-01430-X
Library of Congress Control Number: 2011936507
First printing 2011. Printed in the United States of America.

OXMOOR HOUSE
VP, PUBLISHING DIRECTOR: Jim Childs
EDITORIAL DIRECTOR: Susan Payne Dobbs
CREATIVE DIRECTOR: Felicity Keane
BRAND MANAGER: Fonda Hitchcock
MANAGING EDITOR: Laurie S. Herr

SUNSET PUBLISHING
PRESIDENT: Barb Newton
VP, EDITOR-IN-CHIEF: Katie Tamony
CREATIVE DIRECTOR: Mia Daminato

Outdoor Design & Build Guide: *Garden Pools, Fountains & Waterfalls*
CONTRIBUTORS
MANAGING EDITOR: Bridget Biscotti Bradley
PHOTO EDITOR: Philippine Scali
DESIGN AND PRODUCTION: Suzanne Scott
PRODUCTION SPECIALIST: Linda M. Bouchard
PRODUCTION ASSISTANT: Danielle Johnson
ILLUSTRATOR: Damien Scogin
PROOFREADER: John Edmonds
PROJECT EDITOR: Sarah H. Doss
INDEXER: Marjorie Joy
TECHNICAL ADVISER: Scott Gibson
IMAGING SPECIALIST: Kimberley Navabpour
SERIES DESIGN: Susan Scandrett

To order additional publications, call 1-800-765-6400
For more books to enrich your life, visit **oxmoorhouse.com**
Visit Sunset online at **sunset.com**
For the most comprehensive selection of Sunset books, visit **sunsetbooks.com**
For more exciting home and garden ideas, visit **myhomeideas.com**

IMPORTANT SAFETY WARNING—PLEASE READ

Almost any home-improvement or do-it-yourself project involves risk of some sort. This book is intended as a general reference book only and is not meant to take the place of advice from a home-improvement professional. Time Home Entertainment Inc. and the writers and editors of this book have made every effort to make the instructions contained herein as accurate and complete as possible. However, neither the publisher nor the writers or editors of this book shall assume any responsibility for any injuries, damage, liability, or losses that may be incurred as a result of any project that you may choose to undertake. Tools, materials, and skill levels will vary, as will local conditions at your project site. Therefore, please always read and follow the manufacturer's instructions in the use of any tools and materials, check and follow your local building codes and all other applicable laws and regulations, and be sure to observe all customary safety precautions. When in doubt, or for more guidance on these or any other home-improvement projects, we strongly recommend that you consult a professional about your specific home-improvement or do-it-yourself project.

contents

Inspiration

How to Build

page 68

Here you'll discover extensive step-by-step instructions, drawings, and photographs that introduce a variety of water garden projects:

Finishing the Look

page 98

Refer to this chapter to learn about the latest options in materials and maintenance, plus fish and plants.

Inspiration

A water garden is an essential landscape design element, whether it takes the form of a simple stone fountain bubbling serenely in the corner of a patio or a naturalistic pond stocked with brilliant koi fish and lush, moisture-loving plants. Water in motion is nearly always dramatic, and a flowing fountain introduces water as the star performer in the garden scene.

Quiet reflecting pools, dancing waterfalls, and sparkling streams are just some of the many forms water can take in a residential landscape. Whether it reflects the sky and clouds above, mirrors a piece of garden sculpture, or turns the image of swaying branches into an impressionistic scene on its surface, a garden pool is visually dynamic and ever-changing. The cooling effect of a fountain or waterfall, especially on a hot afternoon or sultry evening, is as welcome today as in times past. A water garden opens up a whole new world of possibilities that draws you outdoors. And when the weather is less than perfect, a garden pool is the ideal focal point to be enjoyed from inside your home, framed by a picture window or glass door. In this chapter, you will find countless ideas and inspiration for adding water—pools, fountains, and waterfalls—to your backyard. You'll also learn from *Sunset*'s landscaping experts, who share design tips and practical construction details to make your project a success.

Water's allure enhances any garden setting—large or small. Even a small spill fountain in a recessed pool, as shown here, provides sensory satisfaction. When it is incorporated with a functional space such as a stone patio, its use is all the more effective.

why water?

LEFT:
Emotional: Water appeals to and nurtures our senses. In the garden, we respond to the sight, sound and touch of water around us. Even ripples caused by a breeze moving across the surface of a pool or pond are a reminder of the powerful element of water.

BELOW LEFT:
Environmental: People of all ages are drawn to water. Who can resist the urge to dangle bare toes in a cool stream or to gaze at the flicker of bright orange fish beneath the glassy surface of a pond? Adding water to our surroundings enhances and expands our quality of life.

BELOW RIGHT:
Physical: Animals and plants require water to stay alive. The same can be said of humans, although our dependence on water is more complex. Yet there is no denying the satisfying physical response we have to water in our lives.

Artistic: When paired with architecture, sculpture, or ornamentation, water's fluid, transparent character is artful and ethereal. Water's effect improves plants, color, and structure to create an unforgettable work of art in the landscape.

naturalistic
pools

This pool's simple lines echo those of the Japanese tea house nearby. Boulders along the perimeter of the pool are extended over the water's edge as natural outcroppings, although they are mortared in place on top of a poured concrete lining.

RIGHT: This large natural pond is settled comfortably in a spacious landscape, reflecting the branches of taller trees. The scale of this body of water can accommodate massed plantings such as water irises and hostas.

BELOW: A small pool is encircled by native stone, yet the rock edging is nearly obscured by a variety of moisture-loving plants, including clumps of primula, which grow happily in damp spots. As a result, the woodland pool feels timeless, as if it has stood here for generations.

TOP LEFT: This creative installation of a stone-edged pond, positioned just outside the living room, is an ambitious but effective way to move water closer to the home. The partially extended flooring creates the illusion that the house is floating over the water's surface.

TOP RIGHT: There's something visually refreshing about a pool installed in the center or at the edge of a grassy lawn. It's a good idea to use flat edging stone where the pool's outline meets turf in order to prevent tripping and to make the grass easier to mow.

LEFT: This small rocky pool was built with a shallow, rigid liner. The rim's edge is hidden by irregularly sized stones. As ground covers, perennials, and grasses around the pond mature and sprawl, they enhance the natural appearance of the stone.

RIGHT: Add a pebbled shore or a low wooden dock and your pool becomes a swimming hole. This rustic design gains a touch of style with the larger-than-life-size dragonfly sculpture hovering above the water.

This fountain spills over a low wall and into a rectangular pool. Both the centered pathway and the coping that outlines it are cut from the same stone. The formality of the decomposed granite garden floor and the stone pool is enlivened by the use of tropical foliage plants.

ABOVE: The Moorish-inspired outline of this small pool is a fitting treatment for the Mediterranean garden in which it appears. The pool's shape was adapted from the designs of ancient courtyard gardens, where water served both practical and aesthetic purposes.

RIGHT: Formal pools may be raised above ground level and incorporate a fountain. Here, the hexagonal shape and classical stone-tiled exterior complement the formal garden setting, and the pool itself is an artful focal point.

TOP LEFT: The classic outline of this stone water feature combines a more contemporary spill fountain and a rill. At the center, a raised ledge fits within the rectangular outline, creating a channel for water to flow and recirculate.

TOP RIGHT: The smooth alabaster stone, symmetrical planting scheme, and urn positioned at the terminus reinforce the modern formality of this design.

BOTTOM: Block-cut edging that steps down from the pathways and planted borders has a casual formality.

Divided into two equal sections—a sunken spa and fountain at one end and a lily-pad–filled pool at the other—this rectangular design lends drama to the otherwise informal tropical garden.

recessed
pools

An interesting pattern is formed by alternating squares of wood decking. A recessed pool is installed within the edges of one opening. It is both pool and water fountain, thanks to the trio of circular pipes that spill water from above.

ABOVE: A square-within-a-square recessed pool occupies a niche in a stone patio. A beautiful pedestal fountain emerges at the center to spray and spill water into the dark surface below.

RIGHT: A shallow recessed pool is finished with a brick-herringbone pattern. Wood decking installed flush with the brick edging provides an inviting spot for a garden bench.

reflection pools

ABOVE: Like a dramatic sheet of glass, this rectangular reflection pool captures a breathtaking view of the home's architecture, the landscape, and the sky. The flat surface of the water is contained by a raised concrete pool. The design appears both formal and informal, surrounded by weathered decking in a grassy meadow.

TOP RIGHT: A raised bowl stands on a gravel courtyard, emphasizing the water's mirror-like surface. This is a simple and affordable way to create a reflection pool in a small or larger landscape.

BOTTOM RIGHT:
A reflection pool is
placed ideally within
a private courtyard to
capture impressions of
architecture and plants
in the water's smooth
surface.

TOP LEFT: To create a raised pool such as this, you will need to build forms for poured concrete. The help of a skilled contractor will ensure the success of the pool's decorative outlines. Leave planting pockets along the perimeter for perennials, herbs, and shrubs.

BOTTOM LEFT: A circular brick pool occupies a small footprint but easily accommodates papyrus and grasses. Nearly even with the adjacent garden chair, the ledge of this pool is a perfect spot for placing a book or glass of lemonade. Another benefit of the raised pool is the ease of pond maintenance, because bending or stooping is reduced.

BOTTOM RIGHT: A carved stone vessel is paired with an ancient-looking dragon's head to compose a serene moment in a small Asian-inspired garden.

ABOVE: A raised pool adds height to a flat landscape environment and brings the water closer to the eye level of a seated person. Here, the square design echoes the tailored lines of the adjacent clipped boxwood hedge. The thickness of the pool's sides allows it to double as spontaneous garden seating.

design lesson

>> Since a fully raised pool requires excavation only for the wall footings, it can be a good choice in a yard with rocky or hard clay soil.

bowls, tubs, and barrels

LEFT: A wooden half-barrel is transformed into a casual lily pond in the heart of a perennial garden. Used barrels should be scrubbed clean and lined, both for water-tightness and to prevent leaching before you add water and plants.

BOTTOM LEFT: A water feature doesn't have to be large to make an impact in your garden. Small-scale designs, such as this shallow cast-stone bowl filled with water, stones, and floating blossoms are a quick way to add water to your garden.

BOTTOM RIGHT: A metal saucer gets its own attractive edging with wire-grid cages designed as gabion planters. The pebble-filled sections help stabilize the edge of the water garden and double as a place to add moisture-friendly plants.

ABOVE: A popular option for contemporary gardens, as well as a fitting addition to the vegetable patch, a new galvanized metal agricultural trough holds more than 100 gallons to create an interesting raised water feature.

design lesson

A tub garden requires very little maintenance. Simply keep the water level topped and remove any dead foliage as it falls. Pots of submerged plants can be fertilized with a special water plant tablet when blooming. Add a mosquito-control tablet to suppress insects. This type of product contains a naturally occurring bacterium that kills larvae. Use it as directed by the manufacturer.

containers for water

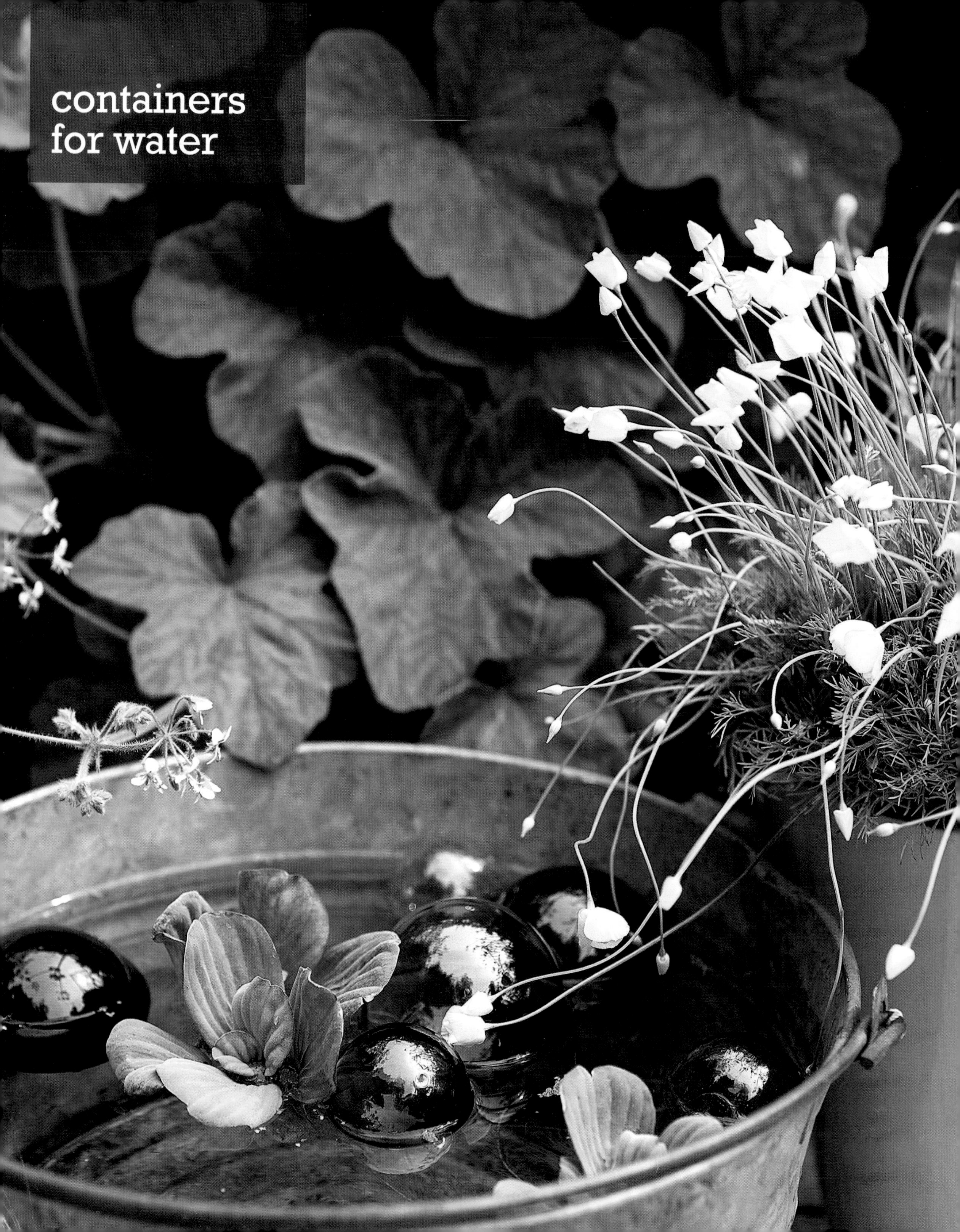

LEFT: No garden is too small for a water feature in a container. Even a repurposed galvanized bucket is transformed into a miniature pond when filled with glass floats and water plants.

ABOVE: The foliage and flowers of just one or two water lily plants are enough to fill the surface of this stone vessel. The rooted lilies are planted inside plastic pots with ordinary garden topsoil and a layer of pebbles on the surface to keep them in place. The plants are arranged at the correct height under the water's surface and can be adjusted with a piece of brick or an upside down pot.

RIGHT: The simplest way to ensure that water gathers in your garden is with a dish rock. Traditionally, this was an indentation in a piece of basalt or granite, formed over time, perhaps by constantly running water. Today, quarries carve or sandblast the surfaces of rocks to create shallow niches. Allow rainfall to fill the recess naturally so that even a small area of water reflects the sky above.

25

tile pools

ABOVE: A stone bowl with a bubbling fountain sits atop two 8-sided tiled pedestals in the heart of an herb garden. The decorative tile design draws the eye toward the fountain. A narrow channel at the base of the smaller pedestal captures the spilling water.

TOP LEFT: Standing at the center of a courtyard, a rectangular pool gains definition from a tiled ledge. The 6-inch-square tiles create a larger pattern that continues along the top and interior of the pool.

TOP RIGHT: An eight-pointed star forms a raised pool with a cast-stone bubbling fountain in the center. Tile wraps around the inside and outside of this Mediterranean-inspired design, echoing tile risers on the adjacent steps.

BOTTOM RIGHT: This elegant water garden combines the benefits of a raised pool with the added style of decorative tile. The size and shape of the 9-inch-square tiles determined both the height and the width of the pool's walls, as the designer did not wish to cut the medallion motif in half.

water gardens

ABOVE: When properly selected and placed, trees, shrubs, and perennials can thrive in and around a water garden. Architectural features, such as bridges, decks, patios, and enclosures, lend structure and stature to the aquatic setting.

BOTTOM LEFT: Flowering water lilies emerge through the surface of a naturalistic garden pool to create a meditative space in the landscape.

BOTTOM RIGHT: A water garden is a beautiful setting for moisture-loving plants and a complement to those established nearby.

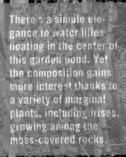

There's a simple elegance to water lilies floating in the center of this garden pond. Yet the composition gains more interest thanks to a variety of marginal plants, including irises, growing among the moss-covered rocks.

SUNSET HEAD GARDENER
RICK LAFRENTZ ON

permits

» Depending on the size of your garden pool, the local building department may consider it either a "swimming pool" or an "attractive liability." You may need to obtain permits and have two or more inspections during excavation and installation. And you may be required to install a safety fence around the pool.

ABOVE: A stone patio is partially suspended over the surface of a circular water garden to create an enjoyable destination in the landscape. The design brings the garden's human occupants close to the scents, sounds, and visual excitement of a water garden.

TOP RIGHT: Lush tropical plants add color, shape, and texture to this naturalistic design. Because most plants require at least four to six hours per day of sunlight, a sunny site is a top consideration when you are choosing the pool's placement.

BOTTOM RIGHT: The entire landscape can be designed to embrace and draw attention to the garden pool. When the water feature is placed where it can be viewed from the inside of a home, such as through the windows of a sun porch, its enjoyment is further heightened.

fountains

ABOVE: Individually and together, water, architecture, and plants play a successful role in this garden. The poppy-colored edifice creates a backdrop for a stacked-stone wall where water spills from an upper ledge into a raised pool filled with irises below.

LEFT: Small fountains make for easy do-it-yourself projects and fit almost anywhere— even indoors.

OPPOSITE PAGE: Whether it spills, splashes, bubbles, or sprays, a fountain creates an inviting soundtrack that enhances your time spent outdoors. Fountains add cooling moisture to the air and help mask neigh- boring sounds so you feel lost in a private Eden. This formal garden is designed around the classic presence of water at its center.

spill fountains

LEFT: An Asian-inspired bamboo spout directs water into a carved stone basin. In turn, the water spills onto a base of pebbles where it's recirculated.

BOTTOM LEFT: Three tiers of weathered steel move water from the fountain's top level to the next. With each drop, the spilling water makes a satisfying ping against the metal.

BOTTOM RIGHT: Spill fountains are designed to capture a specific characteristic of falling water. They create a musical sound depending on the distance the stream of water travels before hitting the pool below. Here, small pipes arranged like rays emerge from two upper bowls, then trickle and splash into the largest bowl at the fountain's base.

RIGHT: Water spills continuously and evenly over the rims of two saucers, collecting in the large pool at the base. This type of spill fountain creates the soothing sound of gently flowing water.

design lesson

A spill fountain requires no more than a spout, a watertight container or vessel, and a pump.

spray fountains

LEFT: A spray fountain uses water in opposition to gravity to create picturesque water patterns, as well as the sight and sound of falling water in a garden. Here, a single pipe emits a jet of water that rises vertically and descends in a graceful arc.

TOP RIGHT: Water shoots upward from a spray head mounted in the center of a raised, brick-edged pool. It then drops to cause tiny ripples to form across its surface

BOTTOM RIGHT: A gentle spray emerges from the center of a trio of frogs, creating a whimsical detail in the garden pool.

SUNSET SENIOR GARDEN
EDITOR JULIE CHAI ON

spray fountain do's and don'ts

In general, the pool diameter should be at least two times as wide as the height of the water spray. The fountain jet is usually mounted just above water level. If your pool will include water plants or fish, plan the installation carefully. Many water plants, especially lilies, do not thrive in heavy turbulence. Fish tend to avoid areas near a fountain, though the aeration provided by moving water is good for their environment.

bubbling fountains

LEFT: A nearly hidden bubbler head emerges from an unusually shaped boulder that has been drilled to accommodate piping. The water jumps upward and then trickles down the craggy surface of the rock before splashing into a pebble base. A hidden tray captures the recirculating water.

BOTTOM LEFT: A pipe was inserted in the center of this ceramic sphere to create a perpetual bubbling fountain. As the gurgling water splashes out of the decorative ball, it streams into a birdbath-style pedestal fountain before making the trip all over again.

BOTTOM RIGHT: The bubbler installed at the center of this tall urn creates an upward gush of water, which then cascades into the gravel before recirculating.

RIGHT: A timeworn millstone gains new life when turned on its side and converted into an attractive bubbling feature. Because millstones already contain a center opening, it's relatively easy to add the necessary fountain hardware without drilling.

design lesson

Bubble fountains typically create a short burst of water, which is a good choice in windy settings.

LEFT: A curtain of water splashes over the wide shelf of a combination garden wall and raised pool, promising something cool and refreshing in the midst of a desert landscape.

TOP RIGHT: Water splashes from the stuccoed tray at the top of a tall, slender pillar. This design is a variation on the wall fountain, but here it creates a freestanding sculpture. The splashing sound is enhanced by the velocity and distance the water falls.

BOTTOM RIGHT: A unique splashing rain effect is created by an overhead pipe that has been drilled with small holes. As the water streams out of the tubing, it splashes playfully into the garden pool below.

wall fountains

LEFT: A single pipe emerges through a brick garden wall to trickle water into a simple shallow bowl.

BELOW LEFT: A single spigot mounted against a saffron yellow wall forms a creative water source for this contemporary fountain.

BELOW RIGHT: Water spills from the mouth of a cherub into a wall receptacle. Variations of this classic fountain include lion's heads, Grecian urns or other symbolic figures.

SUNSET CONTRIBUTING EDITOR
PETER O. WHITELEY ON

the mechanics of wall fountains

Although it may look different, a wall fountain operates like most other fountains: Water recirculates from a basin or pool through plastic tubing or pipes to the outlet. Water can pour directly into the pool from the pipe, overflow from a basin, or spill from a series of shelves or trays.

ABOVE: It is possible to add a fountain to an existing wall with a submersible pump and water pipes, but construction is much easier if the fountain is built into the wall during initial construction like the one shown here. Four square openings in a stacked-stone wall pour water into the shallow pool below.

fish
ponds

ABOVE: Full sun is not desirable for fish, so consider the addition of floating and leafy plants to provide shade. To strike a balanced ecosystem, plants should cover no more than 50 percent of the surface of the water, or fish may not get enough oxygen. Even if your garden pool isn't primarily for fish, a few of them can keep algae under control.

RIGHT: Fish don't adapt well to rapid fluctuations in water temperature, so sunken pools, which tend to have a more stable water temperature than raised pools, may be a better choice. Varying the depth of the pool will offer your fish a variety of water temperatures at any given time.

goldfish and koi

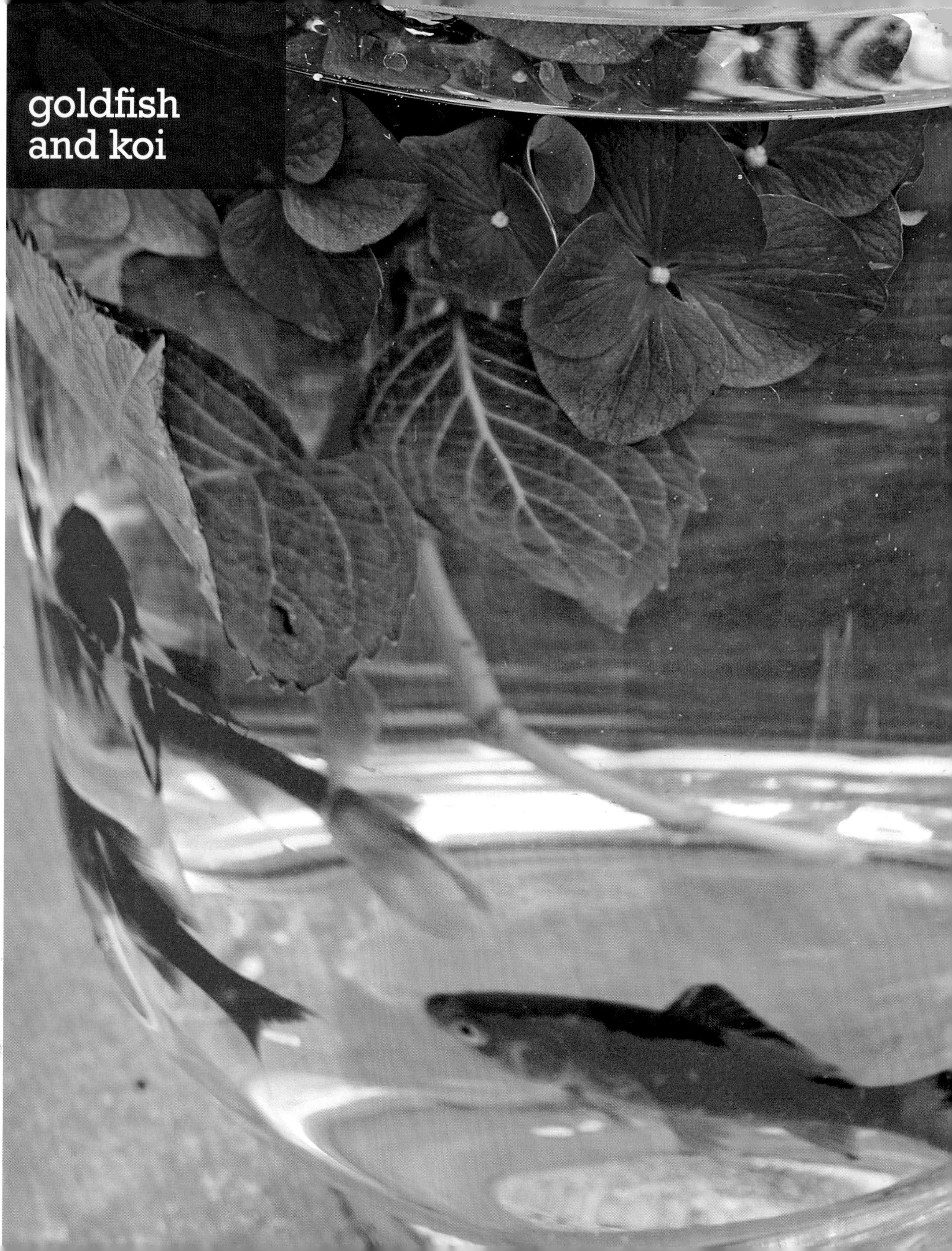

LEFT: Goldfish have been bred for centuries as hobby fish. There are countless types, and they are a good choice for a smaller garden pool. They're normally quite docile and can coexist with each other, although they are not as outgoing as koi.

TOP RIGHT: Japanese koi are actually colorful carp. Bred for their bright hues and patterns, they are also quite friendly—even gregarious. They often take food from outstretched fingers. For success with koi, start with fish that aren't too young or too old.

BOTTOM RIGHT: Gain daily enjoyment from your koi and goldfish by designing a fish pond that is easy to access. The low wood deck that encircles this design allows humans to perch at the water's edge, making it easy to feed and maintain fish and plants.

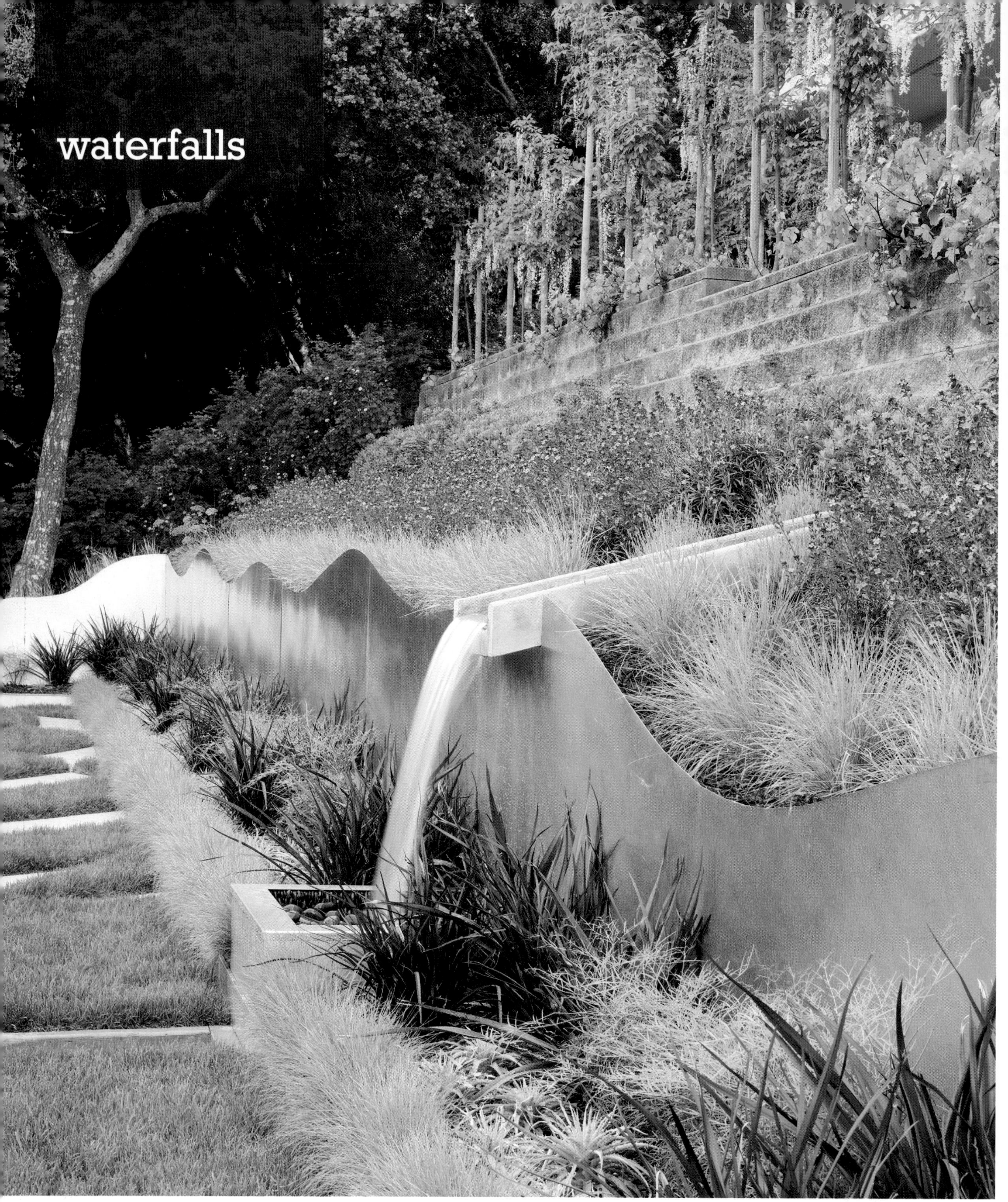
waterfalls

LEFT: Part fountain, part waterfall, this overhanging stream pours into a small receptacle at the base of a retaining wall. The channel through which the water drops is extended beyond the wall by several inches, creating a curtain effect.

RIGHT: A more contemporary fall combines the best of a wall fountain and a dramatic tumble of water. This style is called an architectural waterfall because it uses materials such as slate or concrete and tends to have geometric lines. This is an ideal choice for a waterfall that spills into a swimming pool or spa, where something more nature-inspired would look out of place.

SUNSET GARDEN EDITOR
KATHLEEN NORRIS BRENZEL ON

waterfall styles

>> Before you select a waterfall style, visit nearby parks or public squares and look for ideas to scale down in your garden. Look at natural streams and waterfalls, too; note the way water spills over boulders and meanders between rocky outcrops.

stone and rock falls

SUNSET SENIOR GARDEN
EDITOR JULIE CHAI ON

water sounds

>> Think carefully about the sound you want your waterfall to make. If the flow is slow, you may not hear it distinctly. If it gushes loudly, the presence of water can be distracting to you or your neighbors. You can better control the speed of the water's flow with an adjustable speed pump.

ABOVE: The pace of water that flows through this wide, fast-moving stream is broken up by several short falls placed intermittently to take advantage of the pull of gravity. As water rushes over one rock to the next, the splash and sparkle of the falls add visual excitement to the setting.

A naturalistic stone fall incorporates boulder-sized native rocks, most of which have at least one flat edge to encourage the flow of water. The placement of each rock seems random, which reinforces the appearance that water has emerged from a natural spring at the top of the hill.

ledge falls

Square- and rectangular-cut stones that form this shallow stream and short waterfall match the ledge rock over which the water spills. Each flat rock acts as a step or shelf for the tumbling water. You can adjust the size of the splash and the sound it makes by raising or lowering the stones.

ABOVE LEFT: A ledge-style design creates a contemporary veil of water as it emerges from a horizontal opening in the stone wall.

ABOVE RIGHT: When water is integrated with architecture, color, and plants, it creates an attractive ornamental expression. The versatility of flowing water means that it will complement any design style—from traditional to contemporary.

RIGHT: A stone retaining wall serves an important function in this landscape, but it has an innovative design element with the insertion of a ledge fall at the upper rim. The water spills from here, cascading into a small pool in the patio below.

preformed waterfalls

ABOVE: Instead of piecing together a waterfall with liner and stone, you can buy preformed liners in a number of configurations. Some have steps molded in, while others include a holding basin, filtration system, and spillway. These triple-duty products eliminate the need to create an upper pond for your waterfall.

design lesson

You can often camouflage the edges of a preformed waterfall or prefabricated rocks using smaller natural rocks or carefree, billowy plantings. As grasses, ground covers, and perennials begin to mature and establish, they will make a new water feature appear more natural in your landscape.

This preformed waterfall has the look of an established rock outcropping. Fabricated waterfalls are available in different materials, including lightweight plastic, fiberglass, reconstituted stone, or concrete. As with a natural waterfall, the first necessity is to prepare the soil or hill so it is firmly packed and can support the system you plan on installing.

streams

TOP LEFT: Small, medium, and large rocks form this shallow stream that meanders through a garden. This feature is so casually created that it barely appears to have been placed by human hands.

TOP RIGHT: If you are fortunate enough to have an existing natural stream running across your property, you've already saved construction time and expense. But if you wish to alter the stream in any way, contact the Department of Fish and Game in your state. Established laws govern all changes made to streams, and they are strictly enforced. In most areas, you'll also need to contact county and municipal planning officials.

BOTTOM: This field stream follows the natural contours of a hillside. Whenever you can work with the existing site rather than having to move or excavate soil, the stream or waterfall will feel compatible with the landscape it occupies.

RIGHT: This rustic stream has all the elements that draw humans to the water. There is a cabin at the head, complete with a pole-style ladder. And farther down the stream, a stone footbridge allows passage from one bank to the next.

LEFT: With a touch of whimsy, this garden table planted with vibrant succulents features a rill-style strip of water that crosses the entire length like a table runner.

TOP LEFT: A curlicue-style rill divides a stone patio with a stream of water that flows from a fountain above.

TOP RIGHT: Originally a naturally occurring incision in the soil, often due to erosion, the contemporary term "rill" now refers to a narrow channel through which water flows. This design element can be ancient in appearance, evoking centuries-old methods of moving water, or it can be thoroughly modern, as seen here. A band of water travels between two planted strips and spills through a small opening.

BOTTOM: This stair-stepped rill moves a band of water along the edge of a stone staircase, combining fountain, fall, and rill into one design treatment.

bridges and steppingstones

LEFT: Well anchored underneath so they appear to float over the koi pond, basalt planks are staggered to line up with flat boulders and promise an enjoyable journey over the water.

ABOVE: Nothing is more picturesque than a Monet-inspired bridge spanning a pool of water. The gently arched bridge is supported by solid footings installed well back from the bank. When planning a footbridge, follow local building codes for railing spacing and height.

structures

ABOVE: A classic eight-sided white gazebo has a cedar shingle roof and is fully enclosed with a glass door and windows for year-round use. Also known as a garden house in traditional English settings, this structure is well placed near the lily garden and koi pond.

LEFT: Built from timbers on a small raised dock, a square pavilion provides protection from the sun or rain but is also open to the views on all four sides.

RIGHT: A series of metal French-style arcs form an arbor that spans both the patio and water feature. The openings between each arc are lighter looking than a traditional solid-roof patio covering while still providing shade for poolside loungers.

seating and enclosures

ABOVE: Placed at the edge of a small pond, a rustic peeled-pole armchair welcomes daydreamers.

LEFT: A raised pool that one would appreciate from a distance becomes an inviting destination in the landscape, thanks to the addition of a simple plank-style bench. The tailored lines of the bench are also compatible with the unfussy square pool.

ABOVE: The smooth stucco retaining wall that adds privacy to this courtyard also serves as the back of a cushion-covered bench and the inspiration for an unusual rill-style fountain that extends toward the low pool. These well-integrated elements add up to a thoughtfully designed small garden space.

design lesson

» For conventional seating, a bench or chair should be 15 to 18 inches high. If there is a back, it should offer support at least 12 inches high. For an inclined back, the most comfortable angle is between 20 and 30 degrees.

dry creek beds

LEFT: This modern take on a dry creek bed has an edgy beauty that suggests a point where flowing water might pool.

BOTTOM LEFT: Sand, variously sized smooth rocks, and feather grass represent what one might see during low tide on a beach. The large and small rocks look as if waves have pushed them into place.

BOTTOM RIGHT: A realistic dry creek conveys a sense of moving water, which always flows in the direction of least resistance. Boulders, gravel, and pebbles are placed so as to suggest that the force of water has shaped the creek bed.

In most streams, there are places where water slows and pools in deep spots, or tumbles and swirls around shallower stretches. This creek bed was designed to emulate what naturally occurs when a stream runs dry.

How to Build

Your personal water world may be modest or ambitious, set into an existing landscape or incorporated into a new garden. Water's presence promises to be satisfying to all of the senses. Perhaps you've already chosen a backyard pool, pond, stream, or waterfall design. And you've selected materials and decided on the plants and fish to add. Now it's time to make that dream into a reality and begin the construction. This chapter will take you through each aspect of the building process for several types of water projects, from assembling the necessary tools to adding water when the job is near completion. Get advice and ideas from *Sunset* experts who help to demystify the process of building these impressive features. We've also included edging and border ideas to define the margins of your pond or pool. And finally, consider the ins and outs of plumbing, electricity, and other mechanics to complete the project and give you hours of enjoyment in and near the water.

A colorful al fresco living room makes the most of a narrow side yard, with each feature serving multiple purposes. Water passes through a slit near the top of a stucco-faced privacy wall and falls through a bed of cobbles into an underground basin, then recirculates.

While this is a small site, the design encompasses a stream and a dry creek bed fringed with grasses, natives such as pink penstemon, and Mediterranean plants such as yellow Jerusalem sage (*Phlomis fruticosa*). A native California grape vine scrambles up the sheltering arbor.

Building a water feature takes time and a commitment of energy, but if it is done right, the result will be more than worth it. To ensure the best possible outcome, don't rush the job. Shortcuts will invariably end up costing you more time and money in repairs and replacement materials down the road. As with any project, follow this advice: Build it right.

PLAN AND ASSESS   Follow this checklist for a smooth project

» **Locate** property lines to be sure your project doesn't cross into a neighbor's yard.

» **Check** with local officials regarding zoning restrictions, setbacks, rights of way, height limits, and permit requirements.

» **Contact** local utilities to determine the location of buried water, gas, sewer, or electric lines.

» **Note** the topography. Slopes drain more quickly, and water may pool in low spots.

» **Identify** existing plants you want to keep, as they may need protection or possibly to be moved to a temporary "nursery" during construction. If a tree or shrub requires relocation, it's best to do this early in the process so you can get a feeling for how the space feels without it.

» **Plan** for access. Large projects may require a clear route from the street for deliveries of stone or a spot to unload gravel or soil. If you are unable to gain access to a driveway as a staging area, you may need to use boards or a tarp laid over a grassy area to protect it during construction.

» **Think** resourcefully about excavation and demolition. Rather than sending excess soil or demolished sections of concrete to the landfill, be inventive about keeping that material on the property. When digging a pond, for instance, consider adding berms, or low planting mounds, elsewhere in the landscape. Repurposed concrete pieces can be stacked to create raised planting beds or used as edging. If you must remove demolition debris, investigate local options for recycling.

» **Draw** a plan of how your project will fit into the existing landscape. This can be a simple sketch or a more detailed plan drawn to scale (see page 77). Another easy design trick is to enlarge photographs of your front or back yard and, using an overlay of tracing paper, sketch new design features around the water's edge, such as walls and pathways.

SUNSET GARDEN EDITOR KATHLEEN NORRIS BRENZEL ON

when to build

» The best time to build a water feature, particularly in cooler climates, is in the spring at the start of the growing season. That way, you can begin planting almost as soon as you have finished construction.

choose the best spot

This area receives mainly dappled light, which also means that most floating water plants would not be happy here. Yet the presence of water is still an important design element, thanks to the raised fountain at the center of the patio and the pool in the distance.

Before you begin laying out a pool, pond, fountain, or other water feature, consider the amount of sunlight and wind the area receives throughout the year so that your design works with nature and doesn't fight against it. You may find that a slight adjustment just a few feet from where you originally planned results in a water feature where plants and fish have a better chance to thrive, the force of wind is reduced, and people will be comfortable during much of the day.

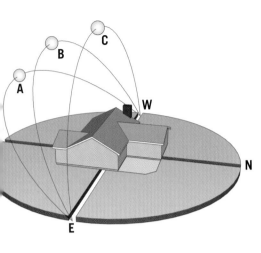

Track the Sun

Calculate how much time each segment of the garden is exposed to the sun to determine your potential enjoyment of those areas. When you track the sun's course as it moves overhead, you can adjust the location, orientation, size, and shape of a pool, pond, or other water feature—and potentially add weeks or possibly months of sun or shade each year. The areas that receive the most exposure to sun during the hottest times of the summer can benefit from overhead protection from the canopy of a shade tree, an awning, or an arbor.

All other factors being equal, the north side of your home receives less sunlight than the south-facing side. East-facing projects are relatively cool because they receive only morning sun. Whatever you build on the west side of your property will receive sunlight in the afternoon, which could make it a very hot space. In warm climates, you probably want to orient such projects on the east and north sides, while in cooler regions, south and west orientations may be preferable.

Also consider the sun's path during the year (see illustration above). The sun's arc is higher in summer and lower in winter, which will alter how light and shadows are cast over each garden area.

Tame the Wind

Observe the wind's course around your home and how it typically moves through your lot. Wind flows like water, spilling over obstacles, breaking into currents, eddying, and swirling. Many garden owners desire a gentle breeze blowing during the hottest times. But keep in mind that gusts of wind can be a problem for pools and water features, since breezes will speed water's evaporation and can wreak havoc on the desired water pattern of spraying fountains.

You can design to protect the water feature from breezes, such as by adding a solid garden wall that is roughly as tall as the dimensions of a pool or pond. Farther away, wind will swirl downward onto the garden floor. A barrier with openings, such as several short walls with gaps or alternating with hedging, will diffuse rather than block the wind and provide protection for a larger area.

More About Microclimates

Nearby buildings, trees, shrubs, and overhead structures create microclimates, so conditions in your garden may vary significantly from those on a neighboring property. In fact, one area of your property may feel different from another area. Certain materials reflect sun and heat better than others. Light-colored gravel, for example, may diffuse or spread the effects of sun and heat, but it can be uncomfortably bright to the eyes.

A shallow octagonal stone pool receives a refreshingly simple spill of water from four spigots on the fountain above. The sound and sight of water can be enjoyed from inside—especially when the French doors are open to the garden.

Where should your new pool or water feature go? An obvious answer: where you can enjoy it. Look beyond the backyard. Consider a dramatic water installation in the entry courtyard, a bubbling meditation fountain outside the window of your home office, or a lush, naturalistic pond stocked with koi and water lilies.

First Things First

Check any deed restrictions, setback requirements, and local ordinances that may affect the placement and design of your pool. In some areas, for example, standard-depth garden pools may legally be defined as a swimming pool. In that case, you might be required to install a childproof fence or take other precautions. If small children will frequent your property, consider a feature designed to prevent accidents, such as a pebble-lined fountain or pondless waterfall with no standing water. Also check accessibility for bringing any supplies or large equipment onto your site. If plumbing and electrical hookups are required, make sure they're nearby.

Size and Scale

There may be both budgetary and physical limitations on the size of the pool you have in mind. Although large ponds are more time-consuming to complete—and more physically demanding if you do the digging yourself—as a general rule, they require less work than small ponds once they are installed. It is easier to establish and maintain equilibrium in a big pond, and fish tend to thrive in larger ponds because the temperature is stable.

Placement Tips

Outlining your pool on the ground with a rope, a garden hose, a trail of gypsum, or landscaper's spray paint will help you envision it. Adjust the outline until the location is just right and the proportions are pleasing. You should also plot out related elements—such as a bog garden or a path leading to the water—at the same time to assess the overall effect. Lay a mirror on the ground to get an idea of what the water will reflect. If you don't like what you see, reposition the pool or incorporate a trellis or hedges as screening.

design lesson

》 Think about your view of the pool. If you install it up a hill, you may not be able to see the water from a patio or first-floor windows. Conversely, the same spot might provide a great view from an upstairs bedroom.

excavating

Edged with native boulders, this natural-looking pond sits comfortably in its setting. It is appropriately sized for the tree-lined property and surrounded by a meandering gravel walkway and an informally planted border.

For small pools and ponds, you may choose to dig the recessed area by hand. More ambitious projects require heavy equipment, such as an earth-moving machine (also called a scooper, cat, or front-loader) available from a local rental outlet. You may choose to hire an experienced operator to do the job, or have the rental company give you operating instructions. Either way, prepare a site where you will place excavated soil before digging commences—ideally, where you can incorporate it into a raised bed or berm rather than hauling it to a landfill.

Making Plans

It usually helps to have the details of your plan drawn on paper before you start installation. Whether it's a simple sketch or a carefully rendered scale drawing, a plan will ensure your pool or pond fits neatly into your desired location. It will also serve as a guide during the construction process. Make a drawing of the area, including trees, plantings, and any patio, deck, or other structure. This will provide an overall idea of the pond or pool setting.

Calculating Surface Area

When you are deciding how many fish and plants to add, it helps to know the surface area. Use the following formula:

Rectangular or square: length x width

Circular: ½ length x ½ width x 3.14

Oval: ½ length x ½ width x 3.14

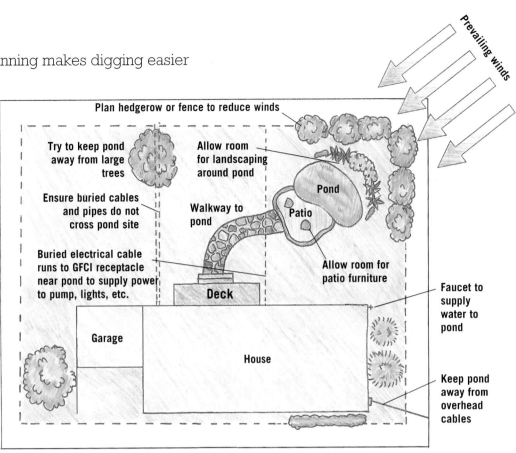

Prevailing winds

Plan hedgerow or fence to reduce winds

Try to keep pond away from large trees

Allow room for landscaping around pond

Pond

Ensure buried cables and pipes do not cross pond site

Walkway to pond

Patio

Buried electrical cable runs to GFCI receptacle near pond to supply power to pump, lights, etc.

Deck

Allow room for patio furniture

Garage

House

Faucet to supply water to pond

Keep pond away from overhead cables

Excavation Plan View

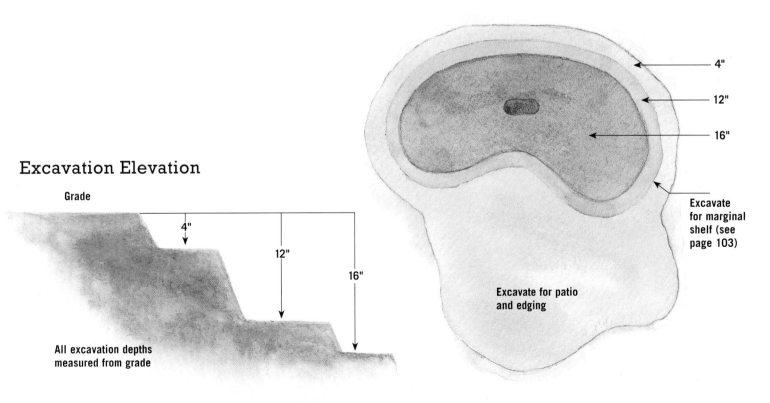

4"

12"

16"

Excavate for marginal shelf (see page 103)

Excavate for patio and edging

Excavation Elevation

Grade

4"

12"

16"

All excavation depths measured from grade

soil
preparation

If you are excavating an area of lawn, keep the uprooted sod in a shady place until the pool is finished. You will be able to use it later for patching bare spots around the border.

The type of soil you have can influence the style of water feature you install. Begin by identifying the soil on your property. The cooperative extension in your community can provide soil evaluation for a small fee. You can also find soil sample kits at home improvement centers. Soil type can determine the ease of drainage in and around any excavation or paving. If your soil is light and sandy, water will drain away faster and it may be easier to dry-set stones or bricks. Heavier clay soil drains slowly and will need more thorough preparation (such as a sub-level of sand and gravel) before hardscaping is installed.

Retaining Walls

Used to hold up a higher level of earth, a retaining wall can be both functional and attractive. Pond builders find them useful to create an edge for a large pond or to emulate a natural waterfall on a slope. Three methods for preparing the slope are shown here:

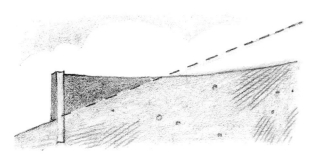

Cut away soil and move excess earth downhill to form a plateau.

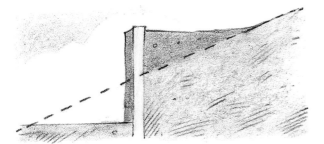

Cut away soil below the wall site and fill with soil on the uphill side.

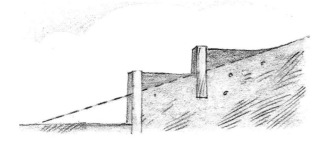

Divide the total wall height into two smaller walls to create terraces.

Stacked-Stone Wall

A low stacked-stone wall retains soil and forms the edge of a small pool. One advantage of a dry-stacked design over mortared stone is that plants can grow in crevices between the stones, softening the overall look.

Concrete Block Wall

Mortared and reinforced concrete blocks hold back earth, as in the corner of this patio garden, to create a clean-edged wall for a tiered pond. Stone coping and decorative tiles complete the design.

slopes

A stone tile wall fountain is recessed in a niche of a rugged stacked-stone retaining wall. The stacked-stone design holds back the upper hillside and also extends the visual impact of the semiformal fountain and pool.

Water seeks its own level, so it's easiest to build a pool on fairly flat ground. On the other hand, slopes create an ideal environment for a dramatic waterfall. You can terrace a slope by placing excavated dirt on the low side to form a berm, or by building one or more retaining walls (see page 79). Once the pool area has been leveled, take advantage of the change in elevation to add a waterfall or stream that spills into it.

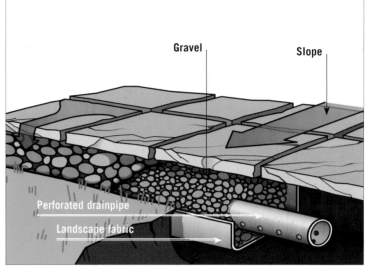

Moisture Management

Whenever you pave around a water feature, its drainage is affected, since water tends to run off even the most porous of paving materials. The natural drainage of a site is altered when you place a large solid object, such as a retaining wall or pond, in the soil. Even this simple flagstone walkway, which surrounds a pedestal fountain and perennial bed, requires a drainage plan.

Drain Construction

If you are planning a large patio to surround a water feature or have soil that drains poorly, you may need to provide an easy way for water to flow safely away. Dig a trench about 12 inches deep (deeper in areas where the ground freezes) on the downward edge of the patio or path and line it with filter cloth (also called landscape fabric). Then add perforated pipe, with the holes pointed down so gravel won't plug them. If your property slopes, extend the trench and add unperforated pipe to carry the water downhill to a point where it can flow out and not pool or puddle. If your land is flat, extend the pipe instead to a gravel-filled pit away from all structures.

Before you cover the pipe, check with a level to make sure all sections slant downhill. Then cover the pipe loosely with additional filter cloth and fill around the perforated sections with round, washed gravel. Cover solid sections of pipe with soil.

Grade for Drainage

Unless the site slopes naturally, grade before you pave so that runoff won't collect where it can cause problems, such as against a home's foundation. Allow a pitch of at least 1 to 2 inches per 8 feet (or ⅛ to ¼ inch per foot). Pay particular attention to grading on any large, impermeable areas; gravel paths on a bed of sand won't need as much attention.

SUNSET HEAD GARDENER
RICK LAFRENTZ ON

permeable paving

》 Permeable paving lets rainwater drain into a deep gravel layer underneath. It's good for the environment because the water slowly percolates through the paving into the soil, reducing storm-water runoff that tends to carry pollutants into local water supplies. Another benefit: no puddles on top of your paths and patios during rainy season.

safety

Even the construction of a small water feature like this requires the use of heavy materials and power tools. Using smart and safe practices while building a fountain or pond will lead to a successful end result.

The rewards of any water feature are earned after the heavy work of building it. For projects large or small, take precautions to avoid injury. Wear sturdy boots and gloves when you're transporting heavy materials, and keep out of the way of a stone that might roll or a wheelbarrow that might tip. On slopes, always begin working from the base and embed each stone firmly before bringing the next piece into place. Start with the right equipment for the project and, if necessary, make it a group project, enlisting the help of friends. It's also important to build well so that the finished design doesn't pose a safety hazard. Consult your local building department about codes as necessary. Hire a landscape architect or an engineer if your site has drainage or erosion problems or if you are building on a steep slope or on unstable ground. As you plan, imagine the finished project. Will children rush to the water's edge? Will the area be used after dark? Are walkways and steps comfortable for people of all ages? Be smart and focus on each detail before you begin. Once you've finished building a fountain, pond, or pool, you'll enjoy its relaxing and soothing qualities—safely.

Lift with Your Legs

Avoid lifting heavy stones into position whenever possible so you don't hurt your back. Drag, roll, tip, or pry them instead. When you absolutely must lift, squat down and grab hold of the stone, then, keeping your back straight and the stone close to your torso, lift with your legs. A lifting belt can help prevent strain.

Use a Ramp

To raise a large stone into position without actually picking it up, make a simple 2 x 12 ramp with 2 x 2 crosspieces screwed to it every 16 inches or so. Carefully roll the stone up the ramp. The crosspieces will keep the stone from sliding back.

Use a Hand Truck

To transport boulders, large stones, or heavy bags of concrete or gravel, a hand truck is highly recommended. A model with air-filled tires is easiest to push and less likely to damage a lawn. Work with a helper to load the stone, then tilt the hand truck back until you feel no pressure on the handle.

Pool Safety

Provide a safe environment around your water garden.

» Monitor children and educate them on the risks of playing in or around water in the landscape. Take steps to protect them, such as building a rock wall around the pond, or creating a wide, shallow edging of plants and pebbles as a "shore," as shown above. A wire mesh placed over the pond or a clear glass or plastic table that sits in the water just under the surface is an extreme measure that will ensure no one falls into the water.

» When installing electrical controls, be sure they are hidden from or out of reach of children.
» To prevent slipping, ensure all surfaces adjacent to the pond provide good traction.
» Check local codes for fencing requirements. When you need to erect a fence around the water, fit it with a childproof lock and ensure it is tall enough to keep neighboring children out of the area.
» When designing the pool, provide a ledge or step around the inside edge to give anyone who does fall in an easy way to get out of the water.

Safety Tips

Always make your personal safety a primary concern when building.

» Wear leather gloves when handling rough materials, and waterproof gloves when working with concrete.
» Protect your eyes with safety goggles whenever there is a risk of flying debris, such as when you are hammering or sawing.
» Remove all jewelry and do not wear loose-fitting clothing when operating machinery like a portable concrete mixer or power tools.
» Do not use power tools around a pond that is full of water.

your tools

If you build your pond with a flexible liner or a fiberglass shell, you should not have to look too hard to find the tools for the job. In fact, you probably already have most of them in your garage. A good shovel is a must. Even if you plan to have soil excavated mechanically, you will almost certainly have to do some touch-up work to sculpt the surface and contour the underwater shelves. Other essential tools are highlighted here. Ensure that your tools are in good working order. Blades should be sharp and handles secure. During the planning stage, make a list of the tools and equipment needed for each step of construction and organize, borrow, or rent them before you begin.

UTILITY KNIFE For trimming liner and other thin materials.

CLAW HAMMER For driving nails; 16- to 20-oz. sizes are most useful.

TAPE MEASURE Available in lengths from 8' to 25'; for all-around utility, 16' tape is best. A locking button prevents tape from retracting, which is an advantage when you're working alone.

METAL BOW RAKE For leveling soil, sand, and gravel.

SPADES AND SHOVELS For excavating, a round-pointed shovel is easiest to use, but switch to a straight-edged spade to make the edges of a trench vertical and to square off the trench bottom. A shovel with a D-shaped handle works well for spreading sand and gravel.

CARPENTER'S LEVEL To make sure all major elements are plumb and level; 2' long or longer is ideal. A line level clips onto taut twine and tells you whether it is perfectly level.

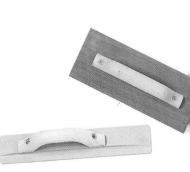

FLOATS A wood float (top) smooths the surface of concrete once it's already been floated with a large bull float, but a magnesium float (bottom) is often easier for do-it-yourselfers to use.

84

EARMUFF HEARING PROTECTORS	SAFETY GOGGLES OR GLASSES	SAFETY MASK	LEATHER GLOVES	KNEE PROTECTORS	DUST MASK	STEEL-TOED BOOTS

ELECTRIC DRILL As well as for drilling holes, this can be used as a power screwdriver (with a special bit).

LONG-NOSED PLIERS Forms hooks on bare wires; cutters can trim, clip, or strip wire. Used to install pool lighting and other wiring.

ADJUSTABLE WRENCH Good for many bolt or nut sizes. Handle lengths range from 4" to 24". A 10" model with a $1\frac{1}{8}$" jaw capacity is good for general-purpose use.

BRICK SET AND MASON'S HAMMER These tools are used to trim small amounts of material at the edges of a flagstone.

MASON'S TROWEL, HAWK, AND BRUSH A hawk (above left) holds wet mortar; trowels (notched and margin shown at right) are used to spread mortar on brick or concrete blocks; and a mason's brush (above right) wipes off excess mortar.

MORTAR HOE For mixing mortar and concrete by hand.

PORTABLE SAW A circular saw equipped with a combination blade can handle both rip and crosscuts; $7\frac{1}{4}$" model is most common. A grinder with a diamond masonry blade trims flagstone much faster than you can do it by hand. If you score to a depth of $\frac{3}{8}$ inch on each side, the stone usually snaps cleanly.

Slate tile walls and a dark base create a mirror effect in a long, slender pool that's both artistic and functional.

Planning, designing, digging, and installing a garden pond or pool is a lot of work. But your project will be manageable when broken into distinct steps. Manage a tight budget by doing the parts you enjoy and are capable of handling. And ease the workload by outsourcing portions of the design or construction to a qualified landscape designer, landscape architect, engineer, or contractor.

Calculating Pool Volume

Deciding on a pump, filter, water treatment systems, plants, and aquatic life all hinges on a working knowledge of your pond or pool's capacity in gallons. Generally, to find a pool's volume, first calculate its area, which corresponds to the length times the width, then multiply the area by the average depth and a conversion factor of 7.5. The trick is finding the "length and width" of an irregularly shaped pond. If you can't find a shape below that approximates that of your water garden, divide the outlines into units of simpler shapes, figure the volume of each chunk, and add them together for the total.

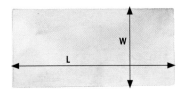

Area = L x W
Volume = area x average depth x 7.5

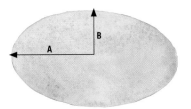

Area = A x B x 3.14
Volume = area x average depth x 7.5

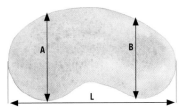

Area = (A + B) x L x .45 (approx.)
Volume = area x average depth x 7.5

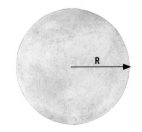

Area = R x R x 3.14
Volume = area x average depth x 7.5

Pond Size

Usually judged by the volume of water it contains, pond size varies from "small," those that hold less than 500 gallons, to "medium," which hold 500 to 2,000 gallons, to "large" ones holding more than 2,000 (see illustration for calculating water volume at left). Consider that future expansion of a small pool will be far more expensive and time-consuming than starting off with a larger design in the first place.

Working with Professionals

Before you seek help, familiarize yourself with the different categories of landscaping pros. Additionally, specialty nurseries and water garden suppliers may offer design or installation services.

Landscape architects are licensed by the state to design residential or commercial landscapes. They can handle a project from concept through completion, producing detailed working plans, negotiating bids from subcontractors, and supervising the installation. If you don't want that much help, you can usually hire a landscape architect on an hourly basis for consultation or to produce a design.

Landscape designers encompass a wide range of people with varying abilities. It's up to you to determine whether the people you interview are qualified to handle the work. Some offer the same services as landscape architects but aren't licensed, though they may be certified by a professional association. They generally have a wide knowledge of plants.

Landscape contractors are typically state-licensed professionals who specialize in installing elements such as ponds, paving, and plantings. Some are primarily designers who became licensed in order to be able to install their designs. Landscape contractors may do the actual work of putting in a garden, or they may hire subcontractors and oversee the project.

Structural and soils engineers are needed when a local building department requires an engineer's stamp on a project. Typically that happens when you're including a structure that will be built on a steep slope or on unstable soil.

edging options

This Moorish-inspired raised pool relies on a stone tile ledge to create its distinct perimeter edging. The design is a perfect complement to the surrounding architecture, art, and plants.

Often, it's the border around the pool that conveys the overall design style and balances with the rest of the landscape. Edgings also serve several practical purposes. They protect the pool from damage, hide liner material, and help keep debris from washing into the water. No matter what material you select, the effect of hard edging can be softened with plants placed along the perimeter.

EDGES AND BORDERS   Select the best option for practical and aesthetic reasons

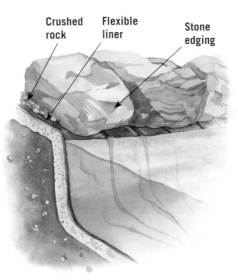

Crushed rock   Flexible liner   Stone edging

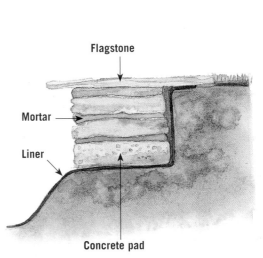

Flagstone

Mortar

Liner

Concrete pad

Choosing Materials

Native rocks and boulders, bricks and flagstones laid in sand or mortar, a grass lawn, an adjoining bog garden or rock garden, a wide concrete lip, redwood or other rot-resistant wood laid flat or upright in columns, terra-cotta tiles, and even railroad ties are some of the many options to edge your pool, pond, or water feature.

Large and Small Rocks

You might dig up these popular edging materials in your own backyard. Stones and rocks look even more natural if several of the largest are partially submerged. In a pond with a flexible liner, achieve this look by digging a shelf around the perimeter. Place the liner over this, set the rocks in place, and trim off any excess. Boulders look best if partially buried or propped up with smaller rocks around which you can pack with soil and plantings.

Flagstones and Bricks

Consistent edging shapes complement formal pools and ponds. For best results, set flagstones or bricks on a 1-inch layer of sand or crushed stone that extends at least 2 feet outward from the edge of the pool. Or the edges can be supported by a concrete foundation. They need to withstand heavy foot traffic. Gaps between stones or bricks can be filled with mortar, sand, or fine gravel, or you can plant grass or other durable vegetation.

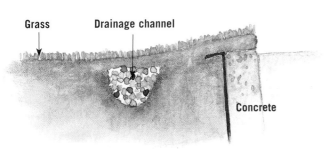

Grass   Drainage channel

Concrete

Grass

Turf is a terrific edging material if you want to soften the outline of your pool. Maintaining grass edging is tricky, though. You need to keep clippings from blowing into the water when mowing. If the grass is in a high-traffic area at the water's edge, you should build in support to prevent collapse. A concrete mowing strip, shown here, helps solve this problem. Build up the grass edge to slope away from the pool's sides and consider digging a drainage channel around the pool. Fill the channel with gravel and direct it to a low point elsewhere on your property.

design lesson

〉〉 Pools don't need consistent edging along the entire perimeter. For example, the more accessible edges can be stone or brick, set on a firm foundation, while the remainder can be formed by large boulders or grass.

pool plumbing

Water spills from a simple pipe to create a continuous, recirculating garden feature. After the fountain drops water into the square pool, the liquid moves via a submersible pump through hidden tubing in order to repeat its course.

Some pools won't need any plumbing at all, or at most a small pump to drive a filter or fountain. Larger structures, such as fish ponds or those including a waterfall or stream, require more elaborate plumbing systems. In the following pages, you'll find an overview of how to choose a pump, as well as details on filters, pipes, fittings, and other pool hardware.

Nuts and Bolts

The plumbing needed for ponds with pumps is fairly straightforward: It comes down to an assortment of fittings, pipes, and valves (see pages 96–97). These are used to connect and control water lines that run from the pump to a fountain, waterfall, or stream head. Piping is also employed to resupply pond water lost to evaporation. Keep in mind that water flows best when it can flow straight. Use pipe with a smooth interior and minimize sharp turns for the most efficient water flow in your layout.

Solar Pump and Fountain

A small photovoltaic panel powers the submersible pump for this pool. To operate properly, a solar panel must be placed in a sunny, south-facing spot near the water. This pump comes with a variety of spray heads that generate gentle streams of water, just right for a small pool.

design lesson

>> In many regions, a modest solar pump plus some plants, like floating duckweed, will keep algae in check and the water clean. Consult a pool dealer or other supplier to make sure your pump is adequate. You may need a more powerful pump with a built-in filter, or even a separate filter. In that case, you will need to access a nearby GFCI receptacle to plug it into (see page 93).

electrical
systems

Underwater uplights focus on the graceful bamboo, while water from the wall fountain adds movement and sound to this courtyard garden.

There are many choices for outdoor lights in your water garden. An opaque covering on a fixture will cast a warm glow rather than a hot spot of light or glare. You can also use lower light levels. At dusk, a little light goes a long way—20 watts is considered strong.

Low-voltage Systems

Low-voltage systems use a transformer to reduce standard household current to 12 volts. They are popular outdoors because they are safer, more energy efficient, and easier to install than standard 120-volt wiring. Light pathways, stairs, the edges of a pool, and even waterfalls with low-voltage systems. You can find a selection of fixtures and kits at electrical or garden pool supply outlets, as well as at home centers. L-V lighting can be purchased as individual components or in a kit that includes a small transformer, about 100 feet of wire, and six to 12 lights. However, by selecting the wiring, transformer, and fixtures individually, you will enjoy a wider selection of lighting designs to complement your garden's style.

Standard 120-Volt Systems

While not as facile as a low-voltage system, a standard 120-volt electrical system offers some advantages outdoors. As with some low-voltage systems, the buried cable and metal fixtures give your installation a look of permanence, but light can be projected at a greater distance than is possible with low-voltage fixtures. If you want 120-volt lighting, it's best to plan for it prior to the pool installation. You may also need to secure an electrical permit. Code guidelines are particularly strict for installations in and near a pool. Installing a 120-volt system is more complicated than low-voltage ones. Cable is usually pulled through conduit, which requires the use of special fittings and connectors. Unless you are quite comfortable with the materials and techniques, leave this work to a qualified electrician.

Controlling Light

A timer will help you manage when landscape lighting and water features operate. If your outdoor circuit begins indoors, you can control it with the same switches and timers you'd use inside the house. But if your system connects outdoors, choose a hardier outdoor timer, as shown above.

Other options include daylight or motion sensors. The daylight sensor is operated by a photocell that reacts to light. When it's dark, the photocell sends power to the light fixture to which it is connected. As dawn arrives, the sensor opens the circuit, shutting down the light.

Motion sensors can be purchased alone or come integrated into a fixture housing one or more floodlights. Some sensors have adjustable ranges and can be set to remain on for varying lengths of time.

What's a GFCI?

To run a pool pump, you'll need a nearby 120-volt receptacle that's protected by a ground-fault circuit interrupter, or GFCI, which immediately shuts off power to the line in the case of an electrical short or power leakage. In addition, all outdoor switches and outlets must have weatherproof covers.

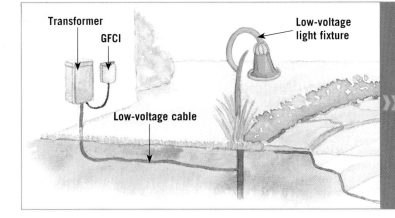

Transformer
GFCI
Low-voltage light fixture
Low-voltage cable

SUNSET CONTRIBUTING EDITOR
PETER O. WHITELEY ON
low-voltage lighting

"Installation is easy. With low-voltage wiring, there is little danger of people or animals suffering a harmful shock. The cable can lie on the ground, perhaps hidden by foliage, or in a narrow trench.

filters
and pumps

A pump serves three purposes: It helps aerate water, adding oxygen and promoting clean water for fish; it powers a pool filter; and it recirculates water to a fountain or waterfall. A pump also allows you to drain the pool in the event of a leak or for routine cleaning and maintenance. Filters help maintain a clean, healthy pool by trapping dirt, algae, and fish waste.

PUMP AND FILTER BASICS The systems that make your project a success

Submersible pump

External pump

Ultraviolet clarifier

Biological filter

Chemical filter

About Pumps

Have a garden pool salesperson help you choose a pump based on the size of your project. You can use the same pump to serve more than one pool feature by adding a T fitting to the supply line, as long as the pump is powerful enough to handle double duty.

Submersible pumps are the most popular choice for garden pools. They sit on the bottom of the pool and are usually quiet and unobtrusive. High-quality submersible pumps have stainless-steel shafts and sealed plastic housings, use no oil, and are quite energy efficient.

» A pump kit (bottom right) includes a pump, filter, and fountainhead. The one shown here is suitable for a small pool.

» An external pump (top right) moves large amounts of water quickly, making it ideal for a large waterfall.

» A large submersible pump (top left) is powerful enough to run water through a pool and waterfalls.

» A pump with an attached prefilter (bottom left) has a simple foam filter that helps keep the water clean. You will need to remove and wash or replace the filter occasionally.

About Filters

Consult a garden pool salesperson for a filter that will work best with your pool. For a large pool with fish, you may choose a mechanical filter that passes water through a box or cylinder filled with activated carbon foam, or fiber padding.

» A biological filter (above left) circulates water through a filtering agent. The filter bed supports a colony of live bacteria that consume ammonia and harmful pathogens and convert them into elements useful for plants and fish. The system depends on a reliable pump that constantly pushes water through the filter.

» An ultraviolet clarifier (above middle) uses ultraviolet radiation to rid a pool of virtually all algae, resulting in crystal-clear water. Both submersible and external versions are available.

» A chemical filter (above right) uses algicides and other water-cleaning agents to attack impurities. This method is often used in small garden pools with no plants or fish.

Pump kit

Pump with prefilter

pipes, valves, and fittings

Water streams along a shallow copper tray before it spills over the edge and into the pool below. The plumbing for this linear design ensures that water flows easily through straight pipes hidden behind the stone wall rather than through a series of turns.

Pipes and fittings allow water to flow in and around your garden pool. Valves let you control the rate and direction of that flow. Most of the plumbing supplies needed for a garden pool can be obtained from plumbing supply stores or home centers. When designing your pipe runs, try to minimize the number of sharp turns in the layout.

LET IT FLOW   Cost-effective and efficient materials for your water feature

About Pipes

Pipes for indoor use are often made of metal, but plastic piping is the best material for most pool projects. Plastic is inexpensive, easy to cut and assemble, and will not corrode outdoors. Flexible pipe is the simplest to work with. Clear vinyl tubing is the least expensive, but black vinyl is stronger and withstands kinks and compressing. Corrugated vinyl costs more than other plastic pipe, but it can be bent around obstacles without kinking, which can reduce the time and expense of installing additional fittings. It can also be buried without collapsing.

If you need to use rigid pipe for an application, choose PVC, which is joined with solvent fittings. White Schedule 40 is the standard, but gray Schedule 80 is stronger and blends in better.

For most garden pools, ½-inch to 1¼-inch pipe will suffice. To move large amounts of water, you may need to use 1½- or 2-inch pipe. Pipe sizes usually refer to the interior diameter, or I.D.

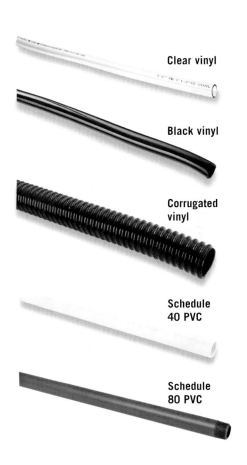

Clear vinyl

Black vinyl

Corrugated vinyl

Schedule 40 PVC

Schedule 80 PVC

Three-way valve   **Check valve**   **Gate valve**   **Ball valve**

About Valves

Valves allow you to control the flow of water to a fountain or waterfall, divert water to a nearby drain, or shut down the entire system for repairs or maintenance. Well-placed valves can make your garden pool easier to use and more enjoyable.

Ball and gate valves are handy for simple on/off use, for isolating a pump, filter, or drain line, and to control flow. Ball valves are considered to be of higher quality. A three-way valve allows you to shut off the flow, send a controlled flow to a fountainhead, or open a line for draining the pool. Need to keep water flowing in one direction or maintain a pump's prime? Install a check valve.

The float valve shown at right automatically controls the level of water in your pool. Once it is attached to a water supply line and installed at the edge of the pool, the valve will top off water lost to evaporation and splash. Hide it under rock edgings or in an adjacent holding pool.

About Fittings

Fittings join pipes to each other as well as to pumps and other equipment. Flexible plastic uses barbed (push-on) fittings and clamps for most connections, while PVC requires glue. Many types of fittings are available. Some of the most common types for pools are shown in the box at right.

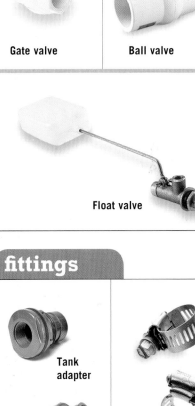

Float valve

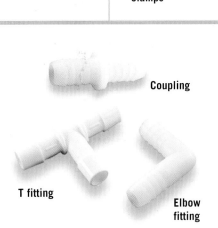

Tank adapter

Stainless-steel clamps

Union

Coupling

T fitting

Elbow fitting

concrete pool

Looking almost naturally formed, this small concrete pool reflects the evening light and lush plants surrounding its edges.

Large-scale concrete pools require you to assemble a reinforced form and work with a large volume of wet concrete. On the other hand, a small free-form pool is relatively effortless—and equally rewarding as a design feature in the landscape. All you'll need are a shovel and trowel and a few sacks of ready-mix concrete, plus perhaps some dry cement color to suit your style.

❶ Dig the Form

As you manually dig shovelfuls of garden soil, you will be shaping the silhouette of the pool. Here, the hole takes on a kidney-shaped outline with some recessed cutouts for placing edging rocks and a small boulder at the end of the project. The sides are gently tapered, and the depth is about 12 inches. If you live in an area with sub-freezing temperatures, add a 3-inch layer of compacted gravel to the form before pouring concrete.

❷ Mix the Concrete

Pour ready-mix concrete into a wheelbarrow and sprinkle in some cement color. Slowly add water, using a garden hose if an outlet is nearby (or a watering can). Mix the concrete thoroughly until it's plastic in texture, not runny.

❸ Shape the Pool

Shovel the concrete into the recessed pool area and work it up against the edges. There is no exact science here; just form a pleasing bowl and round the top edges into an organic-looking shape. Use a rubber float to gently smooth the top surface as the mix begins to set.

design lesson

》 Soften the look of a simple concrete pool to give it a stone-like appearance. On the day after you mix and spread the concrete, you can float some mortar over the surface and sprinkle cement color in a random pattern. Create depth and dimension by adding extra layers to blend and contrast with the original concrete surface. Once you achieve your preferred color and texture, add rocks of various sizes and begin planting moisture-loving ferns or perennials around the margins of the pool.

rigid liner pool

A rigid shell was set in the ground, then surrounded with weathered flagstones. Ornamental grasses make a dramatic backdrop for this small pond, while pink-flowered thrift and sedums grow along the front edge.

While building a garden pool can be time-consuming, it doesn't have to be. The beautiful pool shown here can be built easily in a day or two, and the cost is quite reasonable. Much of the work is already done when you purchase a rigid, preformed pool shell. Simply dig a hole large enough for the shell, edge it with your favorite stone, and chose the plants.

❶ Mark the Outline

First, choose a flat, open area with plenty of sunshine. Remove sod and any existing plants you wish to save. Set the pool shell, right side up, in place. Scratch the outline in the soil with a stake. Then remove the shell and make a more visible outline with sand or flour.

❷ Dig the Hole

Next, excavate a hole 2 inches deeper and 2 inches wider than the shell to accommodate a cushioning layer of sand. Remove any roots and rocks as you work. Use a carpenter's level to make sure the bottom of the hole is flat. As you work, test the fit with the shell. When the hole is ready, pour 2 inches of sand into the bottom and set the shell inside.

❸ Fill and Backfill

Make sure the shell is level and flush with the surrounding surface, removing it as needed to make any adjustments. Start filling the shell with a slow trickle of water. At the same time, begin backfilling by adding about 4 inches of sand around the shell. Tamp the sand down, then add another layer. When the filling and backfilling are complete, pack some extra soil under the shell's lip to support it.

❹ Add Edging and Fountain

Edge the pond with weathered flagstones to hide the plastic lip of the shell. Make sure that most of the stone's weight rests on soil, not on the shell. Set the fountain in the pool, anchor it with stones, and plug it in. Adjust its position to suit your taste. Cover the power cord with mulch or run it through a shallow trench, then add the plants of your choice.

design lesson

》 The owner of this pool installed a solar-powered pump and fountain, which do not require an electrical receptacle. The fountain rests on the bottom of the pool; it's a good idea to anchor it with two or three flat rocks. A standard pump requires a GFCI-protected electrical receptacle nearby to power it.

flexible liner pond

A placid pond brings a glimpse of reflected sky into the garden and offers a cool invitation to take off your shoes and dangle your feet in the water.

Flexible pond liners are easy to install. Stone edging is a good choice for your pond because it serves two purposes: It gives people a secure place to stand, and it hides edges of the liner. If you plan to add rooting types of water plants, incorporate planting shelves—relatively shallow, flat areas—and grow your plants in pots so that the roots will be just a few inches under the surface.

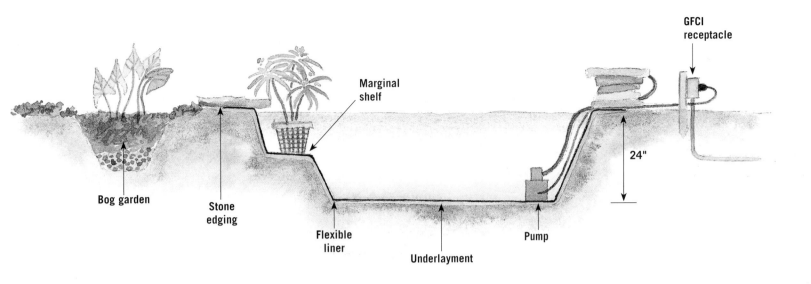

GFCI
receptacle

Marginal
shelf

24"

Bog garden

Stone
edging

Flexible
liner

Underlayment

Pump

How to Do It

For the pool shown in the following steps, the flexible liner allows you to install a fairly large pool in a tight or narrow space. For the project featured here, the liner and underlayment came from a pool supplier. The pebbles and flagstones were purchased from a landscaping source, and a home center carried the pump, tubing, electrical supplies, and tools. The pump needs to be powered by a GFCI electrical receptacle. Plan this before you start digging.

❶ Lay Out the Shape

Determine the outline of your pond. A curving, irregular shape looks most natural and is easier to line than one with sharp corners or bends in its outline. Observe this shape at various times of the day to see how sun and shadows hit the pool, making any necessary adjustments before finalizing the design. Mark the perimeter with a hose or with sand.

❷ Remove Organic Material

Clear the interior of your pond by removing plants or sod. If you want to relocate a plant elsewhere in the landscape, dig a fairly wide and deep hole around it while removing. Keep the roots protected and moist in a temporary location if you need to wait before planting.

continued on page 104

❸ Dig Hole and Mark Depths

Excavate the entire pool area to the minimum depth—here, the marginal shelf that runs along the perimeter. Set aside some of the topsoil to be reused when you need to level the pool edges later on (step 4). Mark and dig the areas that will be deeper, checking that any shelves will be wide enough for plants.

❹ Check for Level

Set a 2 x 4 across the hole and use a carpenter's level to check for level in all directions. If necessary, use some of the excavated soil to build up any low sides. Leave the 2 x 4 in place as a guide to measure the depth of the hole and perimeter shelves.

❺ Add Underlayment

If you're using liner-protection fabric (see design lesson at right), install it first. Smooth the material to minimize folds, and use stones to hold it in place until the liner is added. If the soil is rocky, dig 2 inches deeper and add a 2-inch layer of sand before installing the liner-protection material.

❻ Install the Liner

Drape the liner so that it follows the contours of the hole as closely as possible. Use heavy stones or concrete blocks to hold the edges in place until you are ready to add the water.

❼ Cover the Liner

Spread smooth pebbles over the liner. Do this especially in the shallower areas to protect the liner from tearing should an animal (a heron or raccoon, for example) get into the pond.

❽ Fill the Pond

Begin slowly filling the pond with water from a garden hose. At the same time, start smoothing the liner into shape. Some creases are inevitable, but they can be kept to a minimum with careful fitting and adjusting. Particularly obvious wrinkles can be camouflaged later with rocks or plants.

design lesson

The underlayment material is anything that will protect your liner. If your soil is free of sharp rocks or large, invasive roots, you can use newspaper or recycled carpeting. For more cushioning, use liner-protection fabric designed specifically for ponds.

❾ Add the Edging

With the pond nearly filled, begin installing the edging stones. Trim the excess liner, leaving at least 4 to 5 inches beyond the pond's edge. Add stones so that they overlap the water by 1 to 2 inches. Seat each one carefully so that it doesn't wobble. Use the largest stones in places where people might stand or sit, as this helps to distribute weight away from the pond's edge.

aboveground pools

Raised pools are constructed with the same materials and techniques as in-ground versions, but they create a different presence in the landscape. Visible from a distance and easy to approach, the aboveground pool is an obvious gathering place for one or many. When surrounded by sturdy walls and a wide cap, this type of pool design is also a bit safer, as people are less likely to step into the water accidentally.

This cross section reveals how a rigid pool liner can be transformed into an aboveground water feature surrounded by a 10-inch dry-stacked stone wall. Note how the shallow hole receives a 3-inch layer of sand to cushion and stabilize the liner as it rests in the ground.

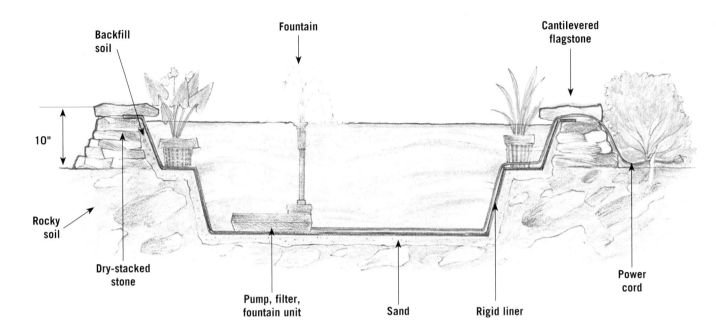

❶ Level the Ground

Draw an outline of the liner to guide your digging (see page 101). Dig a shallow hole to the depth of the liner's base section, plus 3 inches for a sand layer. Dig the sides 2 inches wider all around the liner so it can be backfilled with sand for additional support. Add the sand in the bottom of the hole, tamping it evenly and thoroughly to keep the liner from settling or buckling under the weight of the water. The sand will protect the liner from roots and rocks and help to keep a level base inside the hole.

❷ Place the Liner

Set the liner in the hole and carefully wiggle it around until it reaches a level position. You may need to lift out the liner and add or remove some sand to get it just right. Lay a level across the liner. Start filling the pond with water, double-checking the level frequently while doing so.

continued on page 108

❸ Backfill the Sides

Backfill the sides with sand or the excavated soil as the liner slowly fills with water. Tamp the soil or sand as you work, never letting the water rise higher than the level you're working at—otherwise, the weight of the water may distort the liner.

❹ Install the Dry-Stacked Enclosure

Surround the exposed upper portion of the liner with dry-stacked rocks, using material available from decorative-rock yards and garden centers. Place the first layer of rocks a few inches from the liner and check that it is fairly level. Use extra soil to fill the gap between the shell and the rocks. Taper each stacked layer closer to the liner, backfilling with soil to help support both the liner and the stone. Tamp the soil firmly as you work, and continue to fill the pond slowly.

❺ Adjust the Stones

Chip and break stones, when necessary, for a better fit. Use a stone-mason's hammer, as shown here. If a clean, straight edge is required, cut the stone with a circular saw that is equipped with a masonry blade. (Be sure to wear safety glasses for all cutting and chipping.)

❻ Finish the Enclosure

Build up the rock layers until the surround is even with the top edge of the liner. Mortar a final course of rocks to the top layer, using the longest flat rocks that you have for the cap. You can adjust the height of the capstones by adding more or less mortar underneath. Allow them to hang over the lip of the liner by about 2 inches to lend a greater sense of depth to the pond.

BUILD A STACKED-TIMBER POOL   This aboveground option has a rustic look

Wood timbers are an affordable option and an alternative to building a stone water feature. Built from 4 x 4 timbers stacked and secured together with threaded rods, the project can be assembled in a few hours. You can design it as a square or rectangular pool, using the length of timbers as one guide to determining size. Rot-resistant woods like western red cedar are preferable for this kind of pool, since they stand up well to the elements. Railroad ties and pressure-treated lumber can also be used, but since they are likely to have been chemically treated, take care to protect your water from contact with the wood.

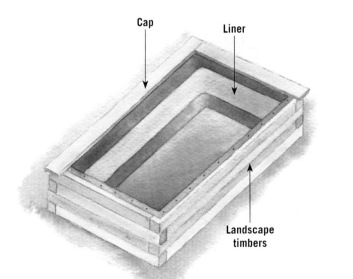

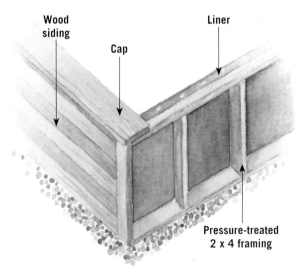

❶ Assemble the Frame

Cut the beams to length for the sides of the pool, following the dimensions of the rigid liner. Dry-assemble the lumber to test the fit. Mark and drill holes through the center of the beams for threaded rods, using one rod at each corner and one at the midpoint of each side. Countersink the holes on the top and bottom of the pool's frame to accommodate the nuts and washers that will secure the rods. The pool can be completely aboveground, or you can first dig a hole to partially recess the pool, line it with underlayment or sand, and then place the shell and frame.

❷ Finish the Pool

A decorative cap trims the top and serves as a garden seat or plant shelf. An alternative construction method is to build a wooden frame that's similar to interior house walls, as shown here. The inside is lined with EPDM or a rigid shell. Cover the outside with horizontal siding, cedar shingles, tile, or whatever material you wish.

Bowls and Barrels

If you aren't up to a larger project, use a tub, bowl, or barrel to create an attractive aboveground water feature—without ever having to lift a shovel. Searching for the right container is half the fun. A wooden half barrel is an attractive choice and easy to find. Large, decorative pots and urns are also suitable. For more ideas on creating a barrel-style water feature, see pages 138–139.

Mortared Stone Pool

This raised pool was constructed with a foundation of concrete blocks, over which cobblestone has been mortared. As a pool material, concrete blocks provide crisp, perpendicular angles and walls, eliminating the need for tricky and time-consuming carpentry forms and pouring wet concrete (see illustration below). A veneer of stone, tile, or brick can be applied with mortar to transform the concrete surface into a decorative water feature. When the wall is complete, spread a liner over the pool or insert a rigid liner. This pool is finished with an attractive cap of ledge stones, which double as a seating wall in the garden. Just add water!

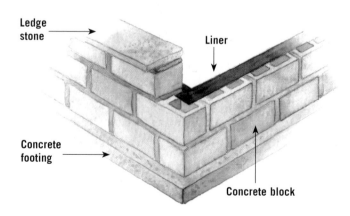

Ledge stone

Liner

Concrete footing

Concrete block

❶ Transplant

Transplant rooted plants to terra-cotta or plastic pots, using ordinary garden topsoil, not packaged potting mix. Spread a ½-inch layer of pebbles atop soil in each pot to keep it in place. Bring plants to the correct height by placing them on top of upturned pots or bricks.

❷ Arrange

Arrange plants to your liking, setting the taller ones to the side or at the back.

design lesson

❯❯ Floating mosquito-control rings contain a naturally occurring bacterium that kills mosquito larvae. To treat a small water feature, break up a ring and use just one-quarter of it.

❸ Add Water

Before filling the container with water, move it to its permanent position. Check that the container is level, then begin adding water. Add a mosquito-control ring if desired (see tip) and tuck in any floating plants. Add water as needed to keep the container full.

spill
fountain

An elegant ceramic urn is plumbed to spill water over the sides and into a plastic bin, where a submersible pump helps to circulate water to the surface.

The quiet splash of water spilling over the lip of an urn or other large vessel can subtly alter the environment in your garden—and improve the mood of those within. The fountain shown here is sizeable enough to create a focal point in the landscape yet easy to assemble in a few hours. Its alluring "music" is created with the help of a plastic basin hidden underground to catch the falling water. A small pump in the basin sends water back to the top of the pot.

How It Works

A cross section illustrates the simple mechanics for assembling a spill fountain. Choose a pot with a slight texture and a color or glaze that looks attractive when wet to emphasize the "sheeting" effect. The pot will need a hole drilled in the bottom (if yours doesn't have a hole, you can drill one with a masonry bit). To catch the falling water, the diameter of the plastic basin that sits beneath the pot should be at least 3 inches wider than the diameter of the pot all around. The depth of the basin need not be more than a few inches greater than the height of the pump.

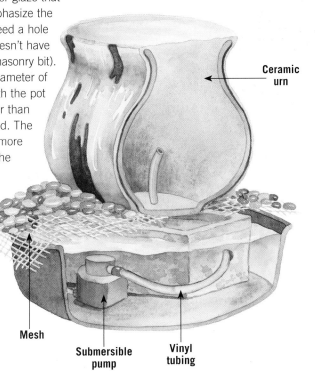

Ceramic urn

Mesh

Submersible pump

Vinyl tubing

❶ Install the Basin

Dig a hole as deep as the plastic basin, and 2 inches wider. Center the basin in the hole and check that the rim is level. To support the sides, backfill the hole with some of the excavated soil. Tamp down the soil and check again to see that the basin is level. Adjust as necessary.

❷ Add a Concrete Block

With a masonry bit, drill a hole for the vinyl tubing in one side of a concrete block. Place the block in the basin (it will support the weight of the pot). Place the submersible pump in the basin. Slide one end of the vinyl tubing over the pump's outlet. Snake the other end through the hole in the block toward the center of the basin; you'll come back to it later. Meanwhile, lead the pump cord out of the tub and toward a GFCI receptacle.

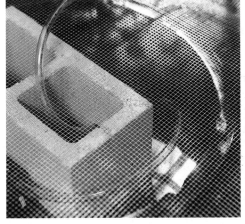

❸ Install Wire Mesh

Cut a piece of heavy-gauge wire mesh at least 6 inches wider than the basin and lay it over the top. Using tin snips, cut a hole in the center of the mesh, making it wide enough for the vinyl tubing to pass through easily. Bend the cut edges of the mesh back so they won't poke the tubing.

❹ Position the Pot

Place the pot onto the mesh, centering it on the concrete block. As you lower, pull the tubing through the pot's drainage hole, halfway up the interior of the pot. Make sure the pot is level. Spread silicone caulk around the drainage hole where the tubing passes through and let it cure. Spread pebbles over the wire mesh, placing most of the larger pebbles toward the outer edges. Trim away excess mesh. Finally, fill both the pot and the basin below it with water, plug in the pump, and turn it on.

Strips of flagstone set on edge form an attractive base for a splashy fountain with the look of a natural geyser.

A fountain, by definition, moves water, tossing it into the air or sending it tumbling over an edge. Besides being irresistible to watch, moving water can make a variety of appealing sounds, from the gentle rattle of a pebble fountain to the gurgle or drip of water spilling on a bed of stones. The instructions here are for making a 4-foot circle, but you can follow these steps for any size spray fountain. Electrically powered fountains require a GFCI receptacle with a waterproof cover, close enough so you don't need an extension cord.

How It Works

No matter what their design, recirculating fountains generally have the same few working parts: an underground basin that holds water and a pump, a ground-level grate covered with decorative stones, and tubing that leads from the pump to a fountain device, such as a spray nozzle or a spout. The water drains through the stones back into the basin. The basin can be anywhere from 18 to 24 inches wide and should be at least 15 inches deep.

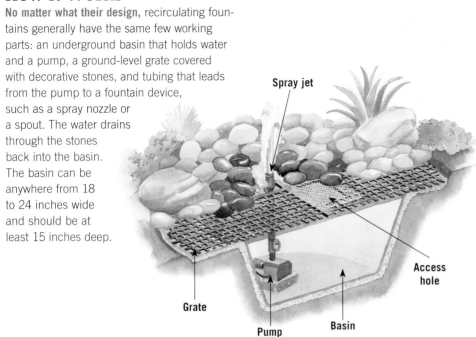

Spray jet

Access hole

Grate

Pump

Basin

❶ Prepare the Site

Mark the fountain's outline and remove any sod with a shovel or spade. Dig a deeper hole for the center basin where the fountain pump will sit, making it slightly wider and deeper than the chosen basin.

❷ Install the Basin

Place a thin layer of sand or fine gravel into the basin hole and tamp it level. Lower the basin into place and check that the rim is level; add or remove sand as needed. To help support the sides, backfill the hole with some of the excavated soil or more sand. Tamp down the sides and check again for level.

❸ Add the Pump and Grate

Place the pump atop a clean brick inside the basin. Pull the electrical cable out and position it in the direction of a GFCI receptacle. Hide the cord and tubing or run them through a PVC pipe buried in the ground. Then place the grate over the basin, making sure it overlaps the edges by at least 6 inches on all sides. Cut out an access hole so you can reach the pump to adjust the water flow or clear the filter screen. Add an oversized square piece of wire mesh to cover the cutout.

❹ Place the Rocks

Fill the basin with water. Place a few larger stones on the edges of the grate to secure it, then cover the rest of the grate with rocks and pebbles. Plug in the pump and check the jet spray. Adjust the water flow if necessary to ensure that the spray looks the way you want it to—and to be sure the water drips back into the basin.

wall fountain

Water splashes from the mouth of a Green Man (also called a fountain mask) into a cast stone basin mounted on a pedestal. The ivy growing up and over the wall hides the water supply tubing, but any sort of vining plant, or even a trellis placed against the wall, will serve the same purpose.

The best wall fountains seem to spout water as if from a hidden spring. Though building one from scratch can be tricky, there's a shortcut: Buy a premade fountain mask and basin of your choice, and then take advantage of an existing wall or fence. Water falls from mask to basin, where it recirculates to the top via a small submersible pump and some vinyl tubing.

How It Works

A cross section illustrates the simple mechanics of a wall fountain. You'll need a wall, of course—plus a pump, some pipe or tubing, and a watertight basin or holding pool. Cover the pipe end with a decorative nozzle or figure, or hide it between masonry units, leaving a narrow slot in mortar or grout. An electrical switch, perhaps located indoors, controls the pump-driven flow, and a gate or three-way valve allows you to adjust the flow as desired. If you wish to automatically top off water lost to evaporation, install a float valve (see page 97) to your water supply line.

Fountain mask

Tubing

Basin

Pump

❶ Prep the Mask

Place the mask facedown on a soft surface. Glue several pieces of cork to the back of the mask to keep it far enough from the wall to allow tubing to run behind it. With a masonry bit, drill an upward hole at a 45-degree angle halfway through the back of the mask, directly above the water spout hole.

❷ Thread the Tubing

Cut a piece of vinyl tubing that is long enough to wind down the wall to reach the basin. Slide an elbow fitting into one end of the tubing. Cut a second piece of tubing, connect it to the other end of the fitting, and push it through the back of the mask's waterspout hole.

❸ Hang the Mask

Using a masonry bit, drill a hole 1½ inches deep at a 45-degree angle down into the wall where you'll hang the mask. Slide half of a 3-inch metal dowel into the hole. Hang the mask on the wall by sliding it over the exposed end of the dowel.

❹ Connect the Pump

With the mask in place, lead the tubing down the wall, concealing it behind vines or lattice. Slide the other end of the tubing over the pump outlet and place the pump in the basin. Fill the basin with water. Plug the pump into a GFCI-protected electrical receptacle.

container fountain

A classic bamboo spout pours water into a glazed basin dressed with small stones and plants. The tiny pump, hidden under the stones, provides the flow.

You don't need a backyard to enjoy a water feature. A small one like this container fountain can turn any space, indoors or out, into a tranquil setting enhanced by the sounds of trickling water. All you need are an attractive container with a wide opening, a pump small enough to fit inside, a spout, a little tubing, and some other amenities of your choice. This project features a variation on the traditional Japanese design called the *shishi-odoshi*, or "deer scarer." Since bamboo is mostly hollow, you can easily make a bamboo pipe and spout yourself, though you may need to do some drilling to hollow it out completely. Tie the pieces together using decorative twine or copper wire. Or purchase a preassembled bamboo fountain from a nursery or pool supply source.

❶ Prepare the Container and Pump

Make sure your container is watertight. If there is an existing drainage hole, plug it with a rubber cork and coat it with a layer of silicone caulk. If the container you select is not watertight, you can apply a coat of acrylic masonry sealer or epoxy paint to the inside. Attach a piece of clear vinyl tubing to the pump outlet. Place the pump on the bottom of a clean container. Add clean rocks around it to hold it in place.

❷ Add the Plant and Rocks

Choose a plant that grows in water, like the miniature umbrella plant shown here. Place it in a submersible dish. The bonsai dish was chosen to add color because it will be visible, but any kind will do. Place the plant dish on the bottom of the container and snake the pump's power cord behind it. Add more rocks to hold everything in place.

❸ Install the Fountain

Thread the tubing up through the bamboo and place the bamboo on the edge of the container. Then pull the rest of the tubing through, cut off any excess, and attach the spout. Aim the spout toward the spot you want to hit with water.

❹ Add Water and Test

Arrange some flat pieces of slate or flagstone on top of the rocks. Fill the container with water—the water level needs to be only slightly higher than the pump. Plug in the pump and check that the water moves smoothly through the tubing. Whenever the pump makes a humming sound, check the water level and add as needed.

Boulder Fountain

Some stone suppliers sell boulders already drilled for a fountain pipe, or will custom-drill a boulder that you select (drilling a long masonry hole by yourself can be challenging). A few smooth stacked rocks and moisture-loving perennials planted nearby complete the design.

Assembly is similar to that of the spray fountain shown on page 114, except you need to pile concrete blocks inside the basin as supports beneath the boulder.

Cushion the bottom of the basin by adding liner protection fabric or scraps of liner. If you want the fountain to gurgle and bubble rather than spray, don't install a spray fitting at the end of the pipe. If you want droplets, add a nozzle.

SUNSET CONTRIBUTING EDITOR
PETER O. WHITELEY ON

low-voltage pumps

Water pumps may be either low voltage (see page 95) or main voltage, operating on household current. The low-voltage option is by far the easiest and safest choice. You need only a simple transformer that steps down 120-volt power to a safer 12 volts and enough low-voltage wire to reach the fountain. You can mount the transformer on a wall or a wood stake placed beside the house near an exterior 120-volt receptacle. Keep the transformer at least 12 inches above ground level. Here, the larger transformer with a timer runs the fountain pump, while the smaller one is for a submersible light.

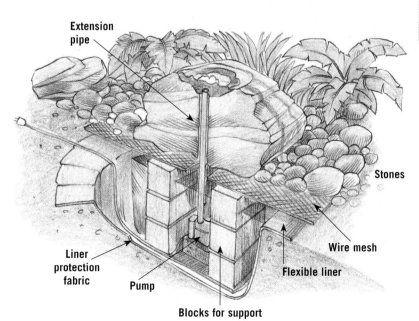

Extension pipe

Stones

Liner protection fabric

Pump

Wire mesh

Flexible liner

Blocks for support

Freestanding Fountain

One of the easiest ways to enhance a yard or patio is with a freestanding fountain. Home supply centers often stock a basic selection, but you will find a wider array of choices from specialty garden centers or water garden outlets.

Freestanding fountains have a water reservoir containing a submersible pump that operates the fountain. This three-part freestanding fountain includes a base, a basin, and a simple spill fountain. Hidden inside the hollow pedestal under the spill fountain is a small low-voltage pump that recirculates water.

Making It Watertight

After confirming that the fountain is level, seal the wiring hole in the bottom of the basin with a special rubber plug that is slit along one side to accept wiring in the center. Slip lighting and pump wiring into the plug, press the plug into the hole in the fountain's basin, and then seal around it with silicone caulk. After connecting the tubing from the pump to the fountain, fill the basin and plug the transformers into a GFCI-protected receptacle.

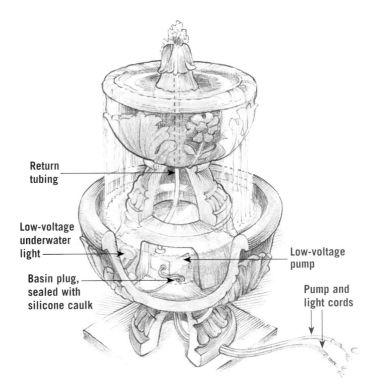

Return tubing

Low-voltage underwater light

Basin plug, sealed with silicone caulk

Low-voltage pump

Pump and light cords

Hiding the Wires

When low-voltage wiring has to cross a lawn, it can be buried without significantly disturbing the sod. Using a taut length of twine to guide you, cut a 5-inch-deep slot in the sod with a square-tipped shovel. Push the handle away from you to widen the cut as you work. When the cut is completed, press the wire down into the slot with a stake. Simply press the sod back together with your foot, and the cut disappears.

waterfall basics

Several spill stones help the water race from one level to the next as it descends the hillside and tumbles into the pool below.

Waterfalls and streams pose some unique technical and design considerations. The primary technical concern is waterproofing. When it comes to aesthetics, only creative experimentation will reveal the most pleasing sights and sounds. Both waterfalls and streams benefit from tasteful border plantings. For planting ideas, see pages 156–169.

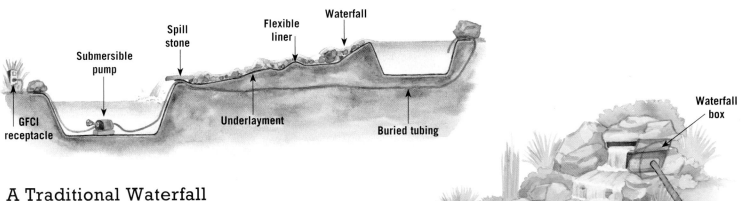

A Traditional Waterfall

This drawing shows an overview of a well-made waterfall. The typical starting point is either a natural incline or the mound of subsoil excavated for a garden pool—perhaps augmented by a retaining wall, sandbags, or other filler material. The entire face of the falls must be sealed to keep water from escaping and to prevent dirt from washing into the lower pool. For a waterproof channel, use a flexible liner, a fiberglass shell, a series of spill pans, free-form concrete, or a combination. Many pros prefer using a plastic liner augmented with mortared stone. Edges of the channels are camouflaged by natural stones and plantings. Rocks and pebbles fine-tune the flow (and sound) of water. Remember that your waterfall should also be attractive when it's turned off. You'll need a submersible or external pump to move water from the bottom pool or holding basin back to the top, where gravity will send it on its way again.

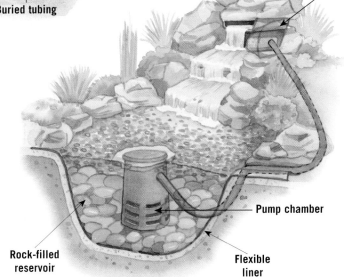

A Pondless Waterfall

Pondless falls and streams fit in small spaces and are safer for children and pets. They are also easy to care for. The key to a pondless design is an underground basin or reservoir that takes the place of the lower holding pool. A pump in this reservoir powers the water back up to the falls through a supply pipe. Water flows over the falls at the top, then down the stream to the base, disappears into the ground through the rocks, and is recirculated. It is basically a larger version of the fountain shown on pages 114–115.

The design shown here uses a waterfall box at the top with a built-in biological filter, plus a lidded pump chamber or vault that keeps rocks and dirt out of the pump. A check valve (see page 97) prevents water in the pipe from draining back into the reservoir when the pump is turned off. Thus the reservoir need not be large enough to hold all the water in the system. The reservoir is filled with large cobbles or rocks, then topped with a layer of decorative pebbles.

simple waterfall

A small waterfall flows along the pebbly and rocky channel, spilling over a ledge to a lower pool. You can adjust the size of the splash and the sound it makes by raising or lowering the stones over which the water falls.

You don't need a huge space—or a lot of skill—to build a pleasing waterfall. (You will, of course, need some strength for lifting and digging.) The simplest, most natural-looking waterfall is a single-step design, with the water flowing from a small upper pond to a larger, lower one. You'll have an easier time creating such a flow on a site with a gradual slope. The pump for this water feature sits in the lower pond. Concealed plastic tubing circulates water from the pump back to the upper pond. If there is not a GFCI receptacle located nearby, have an electrician install one in an inconspicuous spot near the lower pond so you can plug in the pump when your project is complete.

❶ Shape and Dig

Use a hose to try out different pool shapes and falls placement. Once the final layout is determined, mark the outline with bright landscaper's spray paint. Using a shovel, excavate the soil for the holding pool. If you wish, pile up some of this soil to enhance a slope, at the top of which the falls will begin. Shape the slope and water channel using rocks, concrete blocks, or sandbags as needed to give it a step-like effect.

❷ Install a Liner

With padded underlayment in place, line both the hole and the sloping water channel with a flexible EPDM liner. Place the folded liner at the waterfall end, then unfold it toward the pond (a two-person task if the pool is large). Adjust the liner to follow the contours of the pond. Leave the edges untrimmed until after the pond is filled with water.

❸ Place Large Rocks

The toughest part of a falls project is maneuvering any boulders into place, and you may need assistance. Dig out beds for large rocks if necessary so you can settle them firmly into the soil. Position rocks carefully, making sure not to damage or displace the liner. Once the basic structure is complete, place secondary stones, pebbles, and a flagstone waterfall lip, securing them in mortar as needed. Also position some light-colored rocks, which show up better than dark ones, around the edges and bottom of the pond.

❹ Install the Pump and Finish

Attach flexible plastic tubing to the pump. Place the pump in the lower pond and run tubing to the top pond. Fill the ponds with water. Plug in the pump and run the waterfall to check the rock placement and the water's flow and splash. Use a shovel to scatter gravel among the rocks, then brush small gravel pieces into the spaces between rocks with gloved hands. Hose off all rocks to wash away any dirt, pump water out of the hole to clear debris, and refill the ponds.

large-scale waterfall

Installing a pond, stream, and waterfall at once is a significant undertaking requiring planning and hard work, but the results are well worth the effort. While ambitious, this major project will quickly form the focal point of your landscape. When planning the design, consider how it will be viewed from inside your home or from a patio or deck. Take note of potential maintenance issues if adjacent trees are likely to drop foliage, needles, or berries into the pond.

❶ Mark the Layout

Experiment with different shapes for the waterfall, stream, and pond by using a garden hose or rope to mark the outlines. Plan several curves, rapids, and small falls en route to the pond. Sketch each new outline and consider your choices over a few days. Once you've decided, mark the final shape with landscaper's spray paint.

❷ Place the Waterfall Box

Find a location at the top of the stream for the waterfall's reservoir box. Dig the hole until the box is at the desired height for the start of the fall, then dig down an additional 6 inches and fill the lower volume with packed, crushed rock. Install the water-supply pipe connection and the pipe to the back of the box. Confirm that the box is level from side to side and that it's tilted forward slightly. Backfill around it with the excavated soil and tamp it firmly, checking for level.

❸ Dig the Streambed and Pond

As you begin digging, adjust the depth and width of the stream to your terrain and design preferences. To create a louder rush of water, this design has a 2-foot-deep pool directly below the falls. Smaller drop-offs and pools were added to the streambed to supplement the volume of water. You may wish to excavate a few recessed holes in the middle and along the sides as you dig the stream. Later, larger rocks can be set into these holes so that water will swirl around and over their surface.

❹ Install the Skimmer Box

Dig out an area for the skimmer box at the pond's edge. Set the box on a base of crushed rock according to the manufacturer's instructions. Be sure that the box is perfectly level from side to side and front to back. Set the pump in the skimmer box. Install the pool liner around the face of the box according to the accompanying directions. Finally, fit a check valve to the pump's discharge side.

continued on page 128

❺ Build Up the Borders

Working from the top down, install rocks of varying sizes along the streambed to outline the shape and reinforce the banks. Add more soil as necessary to build up the lower sides of stream curves so water will not wash over them. Deepen the streambed as necessary, especially at sharp curves. Fill gaps between large rocks with washed drain rock at least 2 inches in diameter.

❻ Run Supply Pipe

Lay flexible vinyl pipe (in this case, 2-inch diameter) between the water reservoir and the pump in the skimmer box. The supply pipe can be buried in the streambed or run up the side of the garden, as shown here, depending on accessibility. Bury the pipe 6 inches deep to protect it from damage.

❼ Add Underlayment and Liner

Starting from the top, pull the underlayment across the streambed and pond, fitting it to the excavation as you work down the slope. Add extra cushioning over any sharp rocks or roots that could not be removed. Fit the underlayment as smoothly as possible and then install EPDM liner in the same manner. Folds and wrinkles are unavoidable, but try to smooth them as you work.

❽ Hide the Box

After attaching the reservoir box according to the manufacturer's instructions, begin installing rocks around the box to hide it. When possible, mix large and small rocks for a more natural appearance. Place large pieces on either side of the box to frame it, then build up the center section. Rocks can be adhered to each other and to the liner with silicone caulk or black expanding foam (sold at home improvement centers). The foam is also useful to fill gaps between large rocks. Once the foam is injected, press gravel and sand into the material to disguise it.

❾ Fine-Tune the Falls

Many waterfall boxes are equipped with a plastic lip to form the waterfall. For a more natural appearance, fit a wide, flat rock to the lip and hold it in place with plenty of silicone caulk. How far out the stone extends will determine the type of fall you create. For a direct plunge, extend the lip over the pool. Shorten the extension if you want the water to splash down and over the face of the rocks supporting the waterfall.

❿ Add Plants

The last—and most enjoyable—step of any water garden project is bringing it to life with a selection of plants, shrubs, and flowers. Your choices are endless but will be dictated in part by your climate. For a closer look at plants, see pages 156–169.

design lesson

》 Many landscape contractors suggest that a waterfall be constructed no higher than one-third of the overall vertical rise of the stream. Streambeds are typically 2 to 4 feet wide and 6 to 12 inches deep.

dry creek bed

An artful mix of stones creates an eco-conscious landscape feature that works in both dry and lush settings.

Build a dry creek bed that looks as though a rushing stream once moved through and deposited stones, settling them over time. The trick to turning a pile of rocks into an authentic-looking streambed is to arrange them along a slight depression. Construct the creekbed with stones that appear to have been worn smooth by flowing water. Mix together rocks that are large and small or round and flat, just as they would occur in an actual stream. If your dry creek will carry seasonal runoff from rainfall, consider adding some 4-inch perforated drainpipe buried down the center to lead water away.

❶ Mark the Outline

Lay out the design in a natural drainage area, if possible. Use two hoses to adjust the shape and scale so that it seems to meander naturally. Make some parts wide and others narrow. Mark the outline with sand or landscaper's spray paint.

❷ Dig the Channel

Using a spade or shovel, excavate to make the streambed deeper in the center. Use excess soil to build berms beside the bed. (If you're adding drainpipe, dig a deeper trench down the center to house it.)

❸ Line the Bed

Lay landscape fabric over the streambed to prevent weeds from sprouting. Fold and pleat the cloth as needed where the stream curves, narrows, and widens. Place any boulders, setting them into depressions dug 1 to 2 inches deep beneath the fabric. Be sure the boulders are spaced naturally.

❹ Add Rocks and Pebbles

Scatter some of the largest cobblestones on top of the fabric, then add a 1-inch layer of pebbles around them. Toss in the remaining large cobbles and finish with the smallest ones. Walk lightly on the bed to settle the stones. As desired, add plants along the sides of the streambed. Select plants native to your area to make the design natural.

Finishing the Look

You've chosen your garden pool's placement or found just the right location for a koi pond. You've reviewed the necessary tools and building steps to create an alluring water feature. Now you're ready to shop for supplies and materials for turning that design into a reality. Before you begin construction, there are some important finishing details you should consider. You may wish to incorporate lighting in and around the water to extend how you use and enjoy the area after sunset. You'll want to investigate energy-saving systems and evaluate chemical-free maintenance options currently available to pool and pond owners. And, of course, you'll want to choose the right moisture-loving plants to enhance the water's edges or to create an aquatic garden on the water's surface. In this chapter, you'll find a wide variety of inspiring ideas in all of these areas.

Complemented by a tile backdrop, a Cor-Ten steel fountain infuses a modern source of water into a small backyard space. Together, the fountain and pond form a habitat that attracts birds and sustains fish life. For the garden's human occupants, the motion and sound of water offer calming respite from neighboring noises.

Locally quarried bluestone and granite transform a backyard into an inviting outdoor room with water as its centerpiece. Site-appropriate plants and comfortable seating are essential finishing details.

On the following pages, you'll find brief descriptions of the essential building blocks of a garden pool, pond, or fountain. You'll also find brief descriptions of the various types of stone, pavers, and edging for constructing or finishing a water garden project. Details on fountains, faucets, and accessories that channel or spray water are also covered here. Recessed pools or ponds were once made of packed clay or stone. Concrete later became the favored material for shaping pool contours. Some formed pools are still built with masonry materials such as concrete, block, brick, tile, or stone, but today's backyard pool builders rely on two versatile alternatives: flexible pool liners and rigid shells.

Flexible Liners

Readily available at home centers or from mail-order pond suppliers, a liner such as this charcoal-colored option can be draped over many shapes and sizes of excavated holes. Options include:

» PVC plastic, which is inexpensive and commonly available in 20 mil thickness. This type of material can last up to 10 years, although PVC is known to degrade in sunlight and develop leaks. If you are on a budget and not concerned about longevity, this is a reasonable choice.

» EPDM, which is considered the standard liner material. It is more costly than PVC but also longer lasting. It is a synthetic rubber material (shown above) that stretches along with earth movements and climate variations.

Underlayment

Flexible liners should never be set directly on soil. Instead, use some form of underlayment to protect the liner from being punctured by rocks or tree roots. Old carpet or a 1-inch layer of newspaper is often available at no cost and can work well. Sand, roofing felt, and carpet pads are other good choices. You can also purchase underlayment material designed expressly for garden pools.

Other Supplies

If your pool has an unusual shape, you may need to piece the liner together. While a rectangular liner can handle a number of curves and undulations, you can also tape or glue two sections together. Ask your dealer to recommend the right seaming product to construct the liner.

Rigid Shells

Think of a spa or hot tub buried in the ground and filled with plants and fish. Rigid shells are made from ¼-inch-thick fiberglass or polyethylene and are designed to last 20 years or more. They are more expensive than flexible liners but come ready to install. Simply shape a hole that matches the shell's outline, add sand, lower the unit into place, and backfill while adding water. Shells are typically available in round, oval, and kidney shapes. Sizes range from about 12 to 35 square feet of surface area, and most pools of this size are 18 inches deep. Some prefab modules can be joined to make larger units. Others are available with waterfalls and small streams built in.

SUNSET HEAD GARDENER RICK LAFRENTZ ON

buying liners

» Flexible liners come in rolls 5 feet wide or more, but most suppliers will have the width and length you need. To determine the correct size, use this equation: 2D + W + 2 ft. by 2D + L + 2 ft. In other words, add twice the pool's depth (2D) to its width (W), then tack on an extra 2 feet. Repeat this procedure to find the correct length. For example, if the surface area is 8 feet wide by 12 feet long and the pool is a maximum of 18 inches deep, order a liner at least 13 by 17 feet. Ideally, wait until you dig the hole before calculating the liner size and placing your order.

stone
and wood

Often it's the attractive border around the pool that can unify a water feature with the rest of the landscape. You can choose from a wide variety of natural and fabricated materials to build the perimeter, ranging from fine gravels and massive boulders to concrete cobblestones and pavers. Edgings also serve several practical purposes. They protect the pool from damage, hide the liner material, and help keep debris from washing into the water. No matter what edging you select, you can soften the effect by adding plants in and around the water's edge.

Familiarize yourself with the terminology and function of each type of material and then shop stone yards and garden centers to evaluate material firsthand. Home centers and pond suppliers carry some stone and concrete products, but a local stone yard generally has the widest selection.

Choose local or native stone whenever possible, as it always looks more natural than exotic stone shipped from a distance. Local stone is also usually the most affordable option because of lower transportation costs.

Flagstones

Large, flat slabs of varying thicknesses, flagstones are irregular in shape and often have a slightly rough surface. When installed as the sand-set perimeter of a pond or pool, stones should be at least 1½ inches thick. Thinner flagstones will need to be laid in wet mortar or concrete.

Cut Stone

Sometimes called stone tile, this formal-looking material is suitable for a wide variety of projects, including the perimeter of a reflection pool or other symmetrical water feature. Pieces are cut into squares or rectangles (each with a flat back and sawn edges), and the top surface may be smooth or textured.

Cobblestones

Usually carved from granite into roughly uniform cubes or brick shapes, cobblestones are easy to work with. They are excellent as edging material.

Boulders

A general term for a detached, rounded, or much-worn piece of rock, a boulder may be a natural fieldstone that was found buried beneath the soil, a quarried stone that was blasted or excavated from a larger formation, or a large stone that has been smoothed and shaped by water. Use this material to form naturalistic waterfalls, streams, and ponds.

River Stones

These have been tumbled and smoothed by flowing water into rounded shapes. Available in a wide variety of sizes and colors, river stones are especially nice for decorative effects and water features.

Log Roll

Wood decking or a boardwalk can run right up to and over the edge of a pool. Other wood edgings include landscaping timbers, sliced log rounds, upright bamboo stalks, or log rolls, shown here.

container ponds

Water in small measures serves a soothing purpose in a garden, without much effort or expense. With suitable sealing and placement, nearly any container capable of holding water becomes an attractive accent pool. Add your own ideas to the following list: bonsai bowls, terra-cotta planters, wine barrels, industrial drums, claw-foot bathtubs, laundry basins, livestock troughs, glazed ceramic urns. Check a local masonry yard for stones and boulders that have smooth, natural indentations suitable for holding water. Scout for a chipped enamel sink, a rusty wheelbarrow, or even a galvanized bucket. Leave the basin in its rough state or paint, tile, or line it with a mosaic of pebbles, seashells, or found objects. A container pool is limited only by your imagination.

Containers

Ceramic urns are popular choices for container ponds, since they are available in a wide array of sizes and finishes. If the container you select has a drainage hole, you will need to plug it or insert a bowl-shaped liner before adding water.

Troughs

Visit a local feed or farm supply outlet to find a metal trough, either oblong or round, that can hold up to 170 gallons. Agricultural troughs usually come with drainage holes that have been plugged with a rubber stopper. To help reduce water temperature fluctuation, partially sink the trough, leaving a couple of inches above ground to keep stormwater runoff out of the pond.

Half-barrels

Used barrels should be scrubbed clean and lined, both for watertightness and to prevent any substances in the wood from leaching into the water. Smaller rocks and pebbles added after planting will hide the tops of pots containing submerged water plants.

design lesson

›› To create a water feature in a bowl or barrel, select a vessel that holds at least 25 gallons. Almost any leak-proof container will do. If it has a drainage hole in the bottom, plug the hole with a large rubber cork, then seal its perimeter with waterproof silicone caulking. Before placing a wooden, metal, or unglazed ceramic container in its permanent location, coat the inside with epoxy paint or line it with flexible PVC or EPDM. A dark-colored coating makes the water's surface more reflective. Alternatively, you can place the main container inside a more handsome—but less watertight—barrel or tub. The durable plastic liner shown here is sized to slip inside a half barrel.

fountains

Hardy water lilies float in a small entry fountain. The sound of water trickling through the stone orb makes the feature a favorite with birds.

Freestanding Fountain

Freestanding fountains have a water reservoir containing a small submersible pump that powers the water flow. No plumbing is required, but you will need access to a nearby GFCI electrical receptacle.

Ready-Made Wall Fountain

Self-contained, requiring no plumbing, a prefabricated wall fountain includes everything you need to add flowing water to a garden wall, fence, or other exterior surface. As with a freestanding fountain, you will need access to a safe electrical receptacle.

Spray Patterns

Some fountains come as complete kits, while others include the jet or head only and require a riser pipe for the desired height. You can achieve a variety of water patterns by screwing a spray or jet head onto the pipe. Popular spray heads include various dome shapes, swiveling jets, multi-tiered patterns, and spray rings with adjustable jets. Most spray fountains can be powered by a submersible pump, but greater volumes of water may require larger pipes and an external pump.

Bubbler   **Multi-tier**

Tulip   **Bell**

Geysers   **Ring**

Spray Fountain

Spray fountain assemblies include a pump, strainer, valve, and fountainhead (and in some cases lights), all mounted in a single compact submersible base. You pick the pool.

Spill Pan

To build your own wall fountain from scratch, you will need a wall, pump, pipe or tubing, and a watertight basin or holding pool. Many vessel types will fulfill the role of a pan or basin as long as they have been made leakproof. You can also install a flexible liner inside a receptacle to make it watertight.

Water spills from a freestanding section of blue wall and splashes into a small, square concrete basin. Reducing the volume of water also helps to cut energy costs.

Prompted by new energy-efficient swimming pool codes in many municipalities, the pool and pond industry has been developing equipment and systems that lower the amount of electricity used for running water features. Whether you are constructing a new water feature or renovating an existing pond, pool, or fountain, first investigate the eco-friendly options for cutting energy use. Check with the local utility or water district to learn about regulations, and inquire about homeowner incentives, such as rebates for installing energy-efficient pool equipment.

SUSTAINABLE CHOICES
Cut the use of energy and other resources

When constructing a dry creek bed, stream, or naturalistic pool, use stone and other building materials from the nearest source. If you have stones or boulders on your property, incorporate them into your design for a natural appearance. Otherwise, select native or locally quarried rock to reduce the fuel used for transport.

» Reuse old bricks, broken concrete, and other hardscape materials whenever possible. Surround a raised pool with a gabion wall made of salvaged stone or recycled concrete.

» If you have a lawn, reduce its size by adding a permeable alternative, such as a gravel pathway or sand-set pavers. Or replace the lawn with a gravel garden or low-maintenance plants.

» To reduce wasteful runoff when it rains, choose permeable paving materials such as an open-cell system, or steppingstone paths set in gravel.

» Choose low-maintenance and drought-tolerant plants that won't need constant irrigation, pruning, or spraying with chemicals to look good. You especially do not want to use chemicals near a fish pond. Consider using plants native to your area, as they are well adapted to the natural conditions.

» Opt for low-voltage or solar-powered lighting and fountains. Or consider installing new LED lighting in and around water features.

» Set fountains and lighting on timers. For lights, consider daylight-sensitive photocells or motion-sensor fixtures.

» Install variable-speed or dual-speed pumps to run the filter system. These on-demand units greatly reduce the amount of energy used to power your pool.

» When your pool is not in use, install a cover to reduce the energy needed for heating, cut down on evaporation, and minimize maintenance. Use a solar blanket that can be cut to fit to float on the water's surface, or install a costlier (but more durable) retractable cover.

TOP: Native plants populate this woodland-inspired dry creek bed. As the clumps of ferns and low broadleaf evergreen shrubs mature, they will fill gaps and begin to spread over the rocks. These plant choices can typically exist on seasonal rainfall with only minimal water during the warmest months.

BOTTOM: Small boulders and smooth stones collected from the existing property form the banks and give this meandering stream a timeless appearance.

chemical-free options

A growing number of pool and spa designers and contractors now offer chemical-free options. There are several alternatives to chlorines, including saltwater, ultraviolet light, oxidation, and ionization. Each method sanitizes the pool's water in a slightly different way. Since opinions vary on the health benefits, value, or efficacy of each, you may need to do a side-by-side comparison with a local designer or contractor to determine the best system for your needs.

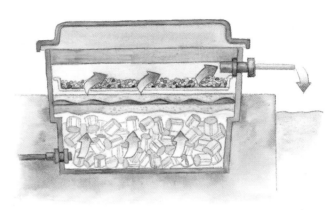

Water-Friendly Plant Care

One corner of this pool disappears into a natural planting scheme, creating a water feature with a dual personality. Especially when plants are installed near the water's edge, it's important to select low-maintenance varieties that do not require herbicides or pesticides.

Mechanical Filter

Mechanical filters use a straining mechanism to trap debris. One type (shown above) circulates water through a box or cylinder containing pulverized ash or activated carbon, zeolite, brushes, foam, or fiber padding. These devices are economical but tend to clog easily under heavy service (as in a fish pond), requiring frequent backwashing or replacement of filter media (or both). Most mechanical filters are powered by a submersible pump.

Biological Filter

A biological filter is a variation on the mechanical theme, relying on pumped water to circulate up or down through a filtering medium. The difference is that the filter bed supports a colony of live bacteria that consume ammonia and harmful pathogens, converting them into nitrates for use by plants and water. The system depends on the constant movement of water, and thus oxygen, through the filter to keep the bacteria alive. A reliable pump is a must. The most popular and easy-to-use biological filters (such as the model shown above) are installed outside the pool and can be disguised by plants or rocks.

Ultraviolet Clarifier

Ultraviolet clarifiers supplement a filtration system to make green pond water clear. These devices kill single-cell floating algae, but not the beneficial side- and bottom-growing algae. Both submersible and external units are available.

Pool Skimmer

A pool skimmer works in tandem with the pump intake to pull dirt, pollen, floating algae, and leaves into the filtration system. The typical skimmer is made from heavy-duty ABS plastic and is housed in a hole dug at the pool's edge. You can set a submersible pump right inside the skimmer. This device is most effective when placed on the downward side of a pool. The wind helps the pump by pushing debris toward the opening.

lighting near water

Since your garden pool, pond, or other water feature was probably designed during daytime hours, you may not have considered its after-dark role. Lighting in, under, and around water can add drama and interest at night. There are several illuminating options, as seen on these pages.

Garden Lighting

Why not string carnival lights so they criss-cross as an illuminated canopy? The lights define a courtyard area at twilight and lend sparkle to the movement of water in a tiered fountain below.

Architectural Lighting

Several types of lighting brighten this courtyard garden. Downward-facing directional lighting throws a wash of brilliance across low, raised walls. Similar up-and-down fixtures are mounted on the columns flanking the pool of water. The water is enhanced by submerged lighting centered under the fountain's flow. Tabletop candles continue the theme for an evening meal.

Up-Lighting

The beautiful form of an Australian tree fern is enhanced by landscape up-lighting, which casts a shadow pattern on the adjacent wall. Underwater lighting draws attention to the fountain's arc as it meets the pool's surface.

Submerged Lighting

Multiple underwater up-lights draw the eye to each fountain's burst of water. Outside the pool, landscape lighting throws a splash of light across the accent boulders—an attractive detail that also makes it safe for passersby.

Modern Lighting

After dark, a cube-shaped raised fountain becomes both water feature and illuminated sculpture in a contemporary garden. Hidden lighting is integrated into the translucent fixture, which is built, gabion-like, with wire screening that contains recycled clear and amber glass pieces. A simple pipe pours water into a receptacle forming the cube's interior walls.

design lesson

Well-placed lighting in and around a garden pool can also address safety, an important consideration. Directional lighting improves pathways, especially where a step or grade change occurs. Lighting can also alert a garden visitor to the point at which a garden border ends and a pool of water begins.

This outdoor dining area has a dual purpose. At its center is a cantilevered steel-and-glass table where al fresco meals are served. Sandwiched beneath the table's glass top, however, is a paper-thin channel through which water flows to spill into a pool below. This is one place where spilled water will not ruin a meal!

Special water effects can enhance the overall outdoor environment, making every conceivable activity refreshing and enlivening. Play with water's role by adding unexpected features. Look for new products and systems that give your pool and fountains something a little unconventional.

Sound Systems

Innovations in product design and manufacturing continue to boost the enjoyment of outdoor water features. Music lovers can listen to favorite soundtracks via waterproof speakers designed to withstand underwater pressure. For example, a party's soundtrack can be piped right into the pool. Wireless and waterproof speakers can project music from iPods or other MP3 devices, bringing tunes closer to the water.

Steam, Mist, or Fog

The theatrics of a cloud rising from the surface of a pool are not for everyone. But in certain settings, the mesmerizing appearance of fog or steam can be a big hit. Swimming pool contractors or online pool system suppliers are a good resource as you start to research the technology options. Special effects are typically achieved with high-pressure underwater jets controlled by a timer. Make sure to see a live demonstration before you commit time and money to add such a feature.

Fire

Placed at the water's edge, a "torch" adds the flicker of a flame in a surprising location. Here, a source of gas powers the half-circle fire. Situated at the base of a flowing fountain, the gas is piped from outside of the pool to a well-protected firebox adjacent to the water.

Outdoor Bathing

Similar to a simple pipe fountain, this poolside shower is constructed from J-shaped metal tubing. The sprayer head is positioned above a saucer-style tray where a bather can stand for a quick rinse. Any excess splashes can simply drain through the spaces between decking.

maintenance and care

This recessed pool with a raised, urn-style spill fountain evokes a serene feeling, although its attractive appearance requires regular maintenance. Anytime a tree—deciduous or evergreen—grows near a water feature or pool, there will be falling leaves, berries, needles, or cones to be cleaned up.

Once your garden pool or water feature is installed, adopt timely maintenance practices to keep it looking attractive. With water in the garden, a seasonal rhythm develops naturally, as it does for other yard maintenance activities. Caring for a pool, pond, or fountain will soon become as routine as looking after the rest of your garden. The payoff is water's healthy presence with fewer cleaning and care tasks.

Leaf skimmer

Wet-dry vacuum

pH treatment

Pond cleaner

pH testing kit

Pool Cleaning Tools

Draining and cleaning require a few simple tools and the regular investment of your time and energy. The equipment shown here is available at most pond supply outlets or online stores.

Spray nozzle

Water Quality

The water in a garden pool should be clean, aerated, and chemically balanced. The chief problem in most water features is caused by an excess of algae, which turns the water green. In a pool or fountain without plants or fish, water can be maintained with a pond cleaner, as shown above. But in a water garden or fish pond, filtration is the important component. A biological filter is most effective when fish or plants are present (see page 145). Some biological filters now come with a UV unit built in. For a quick fix, consider a pond-cleaning product that adds beneficial bacterial to the environment.

About pH

Just as soil pH (potential hydrogen) affects your garden plants' growth, water pH determines whether your pond's inhabitants will thrive. Measure the pH of your pool water before introducing plants or fish, and regularly thereafter. Low numbers indicate acidity, high numbers alkaline. A healthy pool should maintain a pH between 6.5 and 9.5. If you have fish, the range should be 7.2 to 8.5.

Pond Maintenance Chart

	Pond	Plants	Fish	Equipment
Spring	» Inspect liner, shell or concrete for holes or damage and make repairs. » Scoop out leaves and debris.	» Trim dead foliage. » Remove protective netting once marginals emerge.	» Feed fish during the afternoon's higher temperatures. » Inspect fish for disease or parasites.	» Clean and reinstall any pumps and filters removed over winter. » Inspect electrical components and replace any damaged equipment.
Summer	» If needed, clean pond. » Remove string algae. » Monitor water level and top up as needed.	» Add new plants, if desired. » Perform root divisions on mature marginals. » Trim dead blooms. » Remove weeds.	» Monitor fish for illness. » During spawning season, isolate female fish from spawning male fish.	» Clean pump, strainer, and filter as needed. » Install filter if pond suffers persistent poor quality.
Autumn	» Install protective net to prevent leaves from falling into pond. » Inspect pond and make any necessary repairs before winter.	» Trim dead plant life. » Trim tops of oxygenators that have reached top of pond. » Divide bog plants.	» Inspect fish regularly for disease or parasites and treat immediately. » Limit feeding to warmest days.	» Clean pump, strainer, and filter, if required.
Winter	» Turn off moving water features such as fountains or waterfalls, especially in frost zones.	» Lower less hardy plants into water at least 9 inches deep. » Take tropicals inside.	» Install heater to prevent pond from freezing over.	» Prop submersible pumps off bottom of pool/pond. » Drain and insulate unused pumps and filters.

fish pond basics

Lush plants and fish share this pond. Boxwood balls lend structure year-round, while moisture-loving plants thrive at the water's edge.

A fish pond can be almost any shape, though it's best to limit sharp corners or rough edges so the fish don't injure themselves. Adequate depth is even more important. The pond should be no shallower than 18 inches. Ideally, it should be between 24 and 36 inches or even deeper.

FISH-FRIENDLY DESIGN IDEAS   Create a safe and attractive environment

Calculate Volume

A pond must be large enough so the fish have room to swim freely. Figure on 1,000 gallons as the minimum for a koi pond. That translates to a pool roughly 10 feet long by 8 feet wide by 20 inches deep. Goldfish can survive in a smaller body of water.

Establish the Environment

Goldfish live comfortably in water ranging from 50 to 80 degrees, but they prefer the narrower range from 60 to 70 degrees. Koi do not mind a change in water temperature if it's gradual. Water in deeper pools generally experiences less temperature fluctuation.

Keep It Clean

To truly enjoy your colorful fish, the pool water should be as clear as possible. Filters are essential to keep water clear. The best-designed koi ponds often have biological filters and sometimes even a second, mechanical filter—typically, a pressurized sand filter. But even pools with minimal or no filtration can be crystal clear. Water is balanced naturally, as discussed on the following pages. For plumbing details, see pages 90–91.

design lesson

❯❯ A plant island in the center of a pond provides cheery color while offering goldfish and koi a haven from hungry predators.

Slow Acclimation

Before releasing fish into the pool, float them in their plastic bag on the water surface for at least 15 minutes so they will adapt to the pool's temperature. After you introduce the fish to the water, they'll probably take off and hide. Gradually, over a period of days, they should begin to settle in and feed.

home
sweet home

Lily pads and rush-like grasses add botanical interest while keeping the water cool for fish. Just don't cover more than 50 percent of the water's surface with plants, or fish may not receive enough oxygen.

One rule of thumb for stocking goldfish or koi in your pond is roughly 1 to 2 inches of fish for every square foot of surface area. But a better formula is patience. Simply start off with a few fish. If they are healthy, a filtering system is in top shape, and the water is well aerated, you can then add more to your collection.

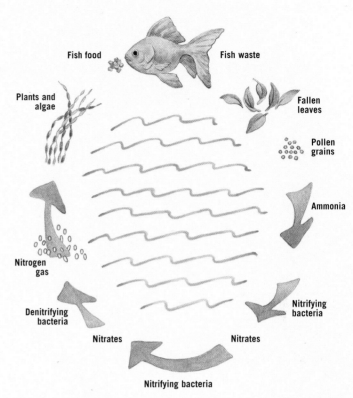

Feeding Fish

Fish don't need to be fed if your pond is balanced, containing insects, algae, and a lot of water plants—all of which fish eat. But if your pond has few plants or if you enjoy the interaction, feed them—just don't overfeed them. Neither goldfish nor koi have stomachs for storing food, so they can eat only a small amount at a time. A good rule is to give the fish only as much food as they can eat in five minutes.

Pool Ecology

"Why is the water pea green, and what can I do about it?" When water gardeners speak of a balanced pool, they are referring to its ecological balance. Algae is the green villain, but in a balanced pool the growth of algae is controlled naturally. Acting in direct competition for sunlight (on which algae thrives), floating plants such as water lilies keep water cool and clear. Small fish feed on algae and on insect larvae. Floating plants, oxygenating plants, and some assorted pool critters are the good elements living in water.

SUNSET HEAD GARDENER RICK LAFRENTZ ON
testing pond water

In addition to pH testing, check your fish pond for ammonia levels. Concentrations of both ammonia and nitrites should be as low as possible. You can purchase separate test kits to specifically monitor ammonia, or a multitest kit that measures both pH and ammonia. To alter ammonia, small water changes are necessary until the readings come down to acceptable levels. Both chlorine and chloramines are toxic to fish. Chlorine will dissipate out of standing water in a few days, but you'll need to take chemical steps if your water supply has chloramines added to it.

planting near water

A s with any other landscape project you will undertake, the best rule when designing a water garden is this: Plan before you plant. Follow the steps outlined on the opposite page for gratifying results.

A well-designed planting scheme gives this small pool its pleasing point of view. The simple elegance of water lilies and calla lilies growing in the water creates a sense of balance with the intense purple blooms of agapanthus thriving in the ground nearby.

PRINCIPLES OF PLANTING   Happy plants, happy gardener

Lay Out the Site

Determine the garden's main point of view. To allow maximum enjoyment of a water feature, situate large-leaved and taller plants, as well as shrubs and grasses, to the rear of the pool or pond. Smaller plants and flowering perennials can be installed in front.

Selecting Plants

Choose plants that will make attractive color and profile combinations and create a feeling of unity in the overall design. Consider the mature size of each plant or tree as you plan its location. A small water feature can easily be overrun by a few fast-growing varieties or eventually can become obscured by a tree or large shrub. Likewise, small plants can be choked by one or two rapidly expanding companions. It's a good idea to reserve at least one third of the garden for evergreen plants, particularly in colder climates.

Plan Your Space

Before deciding on the number of plants, calculate the surface area of the pond (see page 77 for instructions). This information will help you select floating plants. For proper light penetration, and to allow harmful gases such as carbon dioxide to escape the pond, the plantings should cover no more than 50 percent of the surface.

Make a Sketch

A perspective drawing, such as the one shown below, gives you an idea of plant placement inside and around a pond or pool. The different depth requirements of various water garden plants are accommodated with shelves or concrete blocks. For easy removal and for rearranging, plants that root in soil can be kept in planting baskets or buckets. At the pool's edges, a marginal "pocket" resembles a mini-bog-garden. It was formed with the help of a rock dam on the pool side of the marginal shelf.

adding plants

A small, raised pool has the allure of a large pond, thanks to the presence of **vibrant water lilies** and an attractive section of **curly water lettuce**.

Water plants purchased from a local nursery or pond supplier are sometimes suitably potted up and ready for placing in the water. If they are not, you will need to prep them as you would any bare-root plant.

CREATIVE CONTAINMENT   Plant aquatics in pots for best results

Baskets, Buckets, and Pots

Most water gardeners plant in pots, even when it's possible to do otherwise. Pots can restrain vigorous plants. They also simplify maintenance—you just lift the pot when it's time to divide a plant or clean the pool. Floating plants don't really require rooting, but a container will help isolate and control species that may otherwise be invasive. Small pots also help control the spread of oxygenator plants.

❶ Prepare the Container

Line perforated containers with fabric, such as untreated burlap, to keep soil from escaping into the water. With a trowel, fill the planting basket with high-grade potting soil. Stop short of the rim to leave room for the plant.

❷ Plant

Place the plant inside the pot so its roots are inserted into the soil and its crown is exposed. If you are planting multiples, arrange them evenly around the container. Pack the soil firmly around the roots.

❸ Top Off

Add a layer of smooth stones or pea gravel to top off the soil. This will keep the soil from leaking into the water and prevent fish from disturbing the plants.

Container or tub gardens are a pleasing and affordable option, especially if you are limited by space and budget. You need a suitable container, a sunny site, some water plants, and perhaps a few fish to help keep the pool clean. Here are some tips to follow:

» Set the container in the desired final location before filling with water and plants.

» Look for a location that can withstand possible seepage and the occasional need to drain the container. The garden ground may be a better choice than a patio or deck.

» Select a site that receives at least 4 to 6 hours of full sun daily.

» Use bricks or overturned pots to raise planted baskets or containers to the proper height inside the tub.

» Add a goldfish or two. To keep the water free of insects, add a couple of mosquito rings (see page 111).

» Consider a tiny fountain jet, driven by a submersible pump, for visual interest and aeration.

» Drain the container and scrub it thoroughly with a mixture of 4 parts water and 1 part household bleach at least once a year.

encyclopedia of water plants

Even a modest pool can accommodate water plants. Some may float on the surface, while others are contained in partially submerged pots. The result is a magnetic design that draws you closer to gaze and admire the interesting varieties thriving here.

Water plants can be categorized as floating, oxygenating, marginal, and bog (or border). Here is an introduction to a variety of choices in each category. Many of these plants can be found at nurseries and garden centers. All of them, and many others, can be ordered by mail or online. Some suppliers take the guesswork out of plant selection by selling a water garden collection that includes all the plants needed for a well-balanced pool, based on the surface area.

FLOATING PLANTS

There are two types of floating plants: those with their roots in the soil and their leaves floating on the water's surface, and those whose roots simply float in the water. Rooted plants help provide shade and crowd out competing algae. They don't like heavy turbulence, so plant them away from the splash of a waterfall or fountain.

True floaters get their nutrients directly from the water and don't require soil. Most free-floating plants can become invasive, especially in warmer climates, and need to be thinned periodically (some states ban specific floaters, so check your local codes). Keep floaters away from koi, as fish shred the roots, which in turn may clog a pump.

Lotus
Nelumbo spp.
Description: Big, round, green leaves to 2 ft. across. Fragrant white, cream, pink, red, or yellow flowers to 1 ft. wide stand above foliage in summer. **Hardiness:** To −30°F/−34°C. **Planting:** In water to 24 in. deep for larger varieties, to 9 in. deep for smaller ones. Full sun.

Water Clover
Marsilea spp.
Description: Ferns with foliage like that of four-leaf clover; floats on surface, forming carpet. Thin as necessary. **Hardiness:** To −10°F/−23°C. **Planting:** In water to 12 in. deep. Also grows in moist soil, standing erect to 1 ft. tall. Can become invasive; best in pots. Sun or shade.

Water Hawthorn
Aponogeton distachyus
Description: Long-stemmed, strap-like, bright green leaves to 8 in. long. Fragrant white flowers 1¼ in. wide in two-branched clusters above the water. **Hardiness:** To 23°F/−5°C. **Planting:** In water to 24 in. deep. Full sun or part shade.

Water Lily
Nymphaea spp.
Description: Round leaves, deeply notched where stem is attached. **Hardiness:** Hardy types to −40°F/−40°C; tropical types to 30°F/−1°C. **Planting:** In water to 24 in. deep for hardy types; to 12 in. deep for tropical types.

Water Poppy
Hydrocleys nymphoides
Description: Long stems with heart-shaped, shiny leaves to 3 in. long. Bowl-shaped yellow flowers just above water in summer. **Hardiness:** To 30°F/−1°C. **Planting:** In water to 24 in. deep. Full sun or part shade.

Water Snowflake, Floating Heart
Nymphoides spp.
Description: Round leaves to 3 in. across. Small, fringed yellow or white flowers above the water in summer. **Hardiness:** Some species to −10°F/−23°C. **Planting:** In water to 24 in. deep. Full sun.

FLOATING PLANTS (continued)

Fairy Moss, Mosquito Plant
Azolla caroliniana
Description: Dime-size green fern with a single fine root. Turns red in bright sun or cool weather. A few plants quickly form a dense mat. Can be invasive and needs to be thinned out by hand or net. **Hardiness:** To 0°F/–18°C. **Planting:** Full sun or part shade.

Frogbit
Hydrocharis morsus-ranae
Description: Rounded, shiny green leaves to 2 in. across, like little lily pads. Small, bowl-shaped white flowers with yellow centers in summer. **Hardiness:** To 0°F/–18°C. **Planting:** Prefers calm, shallow water. Full sun.

Water Fern
Salvinia minima
Description: Fern with two rounded, stiffly hairy, ½-in. floating leaves like miniature lily pads; emerald green in shade but often brownish in full sun. Submerged, modified third leaf acts as a root. **Hardiness:** To 30°F/–1°C. **Planting:** Prefers still water. Full sun or part shade.

Water Hyacinth
Eichhornia crassipes
Description: Rounded, shiny green leaves to about 5 in. across held just above the water by air-filled stems. Pale lavender blue flower spikes to 6 in. tall in warmer climates in summer. Foot-long feathery roots form spawning areas for fish. **Hardiness:** To 10°F/–12°C. **Planting:** Full sun.

Water Lettuce
Pistia stratiotes
Description: Velvety green, 6-in. rosettes, like little heads of loose-leaf lettuce. Can form a mat several feet wide by summer's end. Long, trailing roots turn from white to purple to black; good fish cover. **Hardiness:** To 30°F/–1°C. **Planting:** Prefers calm, shallow water. Needs midday shade in hot climates.

MORE ABOUT WATER LILIES

These flamboyant floating-leaf plants are the reason many gardeners build ponds. Bearing exquisite blooms over a long period, water lilies (*Nymphaea*) are the showpieces of any water garden. Even when the plant is out of bloom, the lily pads—the rounded, deeply notched floating leaves—are eye-catching.

Most water lilies—hardy or tropical—require a minimum of 5 to 6 hours of full sun each day for the flowers to open. If you have to build your pool in partial shade, choose a location that receives morning sun, or select more shade-tolerant lily varieties.

Hardy water lilies bloom during daylight, opening about 10 a.m., and close after sunset. They are the easiest for a beginner and can overwinter in the pool. Plant hardy water lilies from early spring through October in mild-winter areas. They flower as early as March.

Tropical water lilies, which are larger and more prolific bloomers, must be considered annuals in all but the balmiest climates. With some effort, however, they can be wintered over if stored carefully in a greenhouse or other cozy spot. Although tropicals can be grown in all areas, they shouldn't be planted until average daytime temperatures rise above 65 degrees. Tropicals produce their first blooms in May.

To plant:

» Plant each lily in a container that is about 15 inches wide and 9 inches deep.

» Fill the container halfway with moist soil. Hold the plant in place while adding soil around the roots, firming it in as you go.

» Bring the root crown even with or just above the soil.

» Cover the soil with a 1- to 2-inch layer of coarse sand or fine gravel.

» Sink the containers in your pond. Allow 6 to 12 inches of water above the pot (greater depth limits the amount of light that reaches the root crown). If your pond is too deep, elevate the containers.

» Add small fish and oxygenating plants to minimize the growth of algae.

» About six months after planting, feed the plants monthly with aquatic fertilizer tablets.

Hardy lily 'Comanche'

Tropical lily 'Attraction'

Hardy lily 'Gladstoniana'

Tropical lily 'August Koch'

OXYGENATING PLANTS

These hard workers grow submerged beneath the water's surface and are indispensable to a balanced water garden. During daylight hours, oxygenators take up carbon dioxide and release oxygen to other plants and to fish. Select a variety of types, since their periods of active growth may vary.

Canadian Pondweed
Elodea canadensis
Description: Tiny, dark green leaves on tangled stems. Tiny greenish white flowers in summer. Pinch off old growth or remove excess with a net or rake. **Hardiness:** To –30°F/–34°C. **Planting:** Thrives in cool water. Full sun.

Fanwort
Cabomba caroliniana
Description: Fan-shaped, feathery, bright green foliage with small white flowers in summer. **Hardiness:** To –10°F/ –23°C. **Planting:** Best in warm, still water. Full sun.

Pondweed
Potamogeton spp.
Description: Many species with translucent, seaweed-like leaves. Tiny flower spikes just above the water surface in summer. Foliage provides food and shelter for fish. Hardiness: Some species to –20°F/–29°C. **Planting:** Prefers sun but tolerates some shade.

MARGINAL AND BOG PLANTS

Some water plants do best around the pool's edges, or margins, with their flower heads and foliage waving in the breeze and their feet in shallow water. Most marginal plants prefer water 1 to 6 inches deep. These are the ones that benefit from a separate, adjoining shallow area in your pool or a series of shelves around its edges. Bog plants grow best where splashing pool or pond water keeps the ground continuously moist. As a design element, bog plants camouflage the edges of a pool, waterfall, or stream, lending a natural appearance.

Arrowhead
Sagittaria spp.
Description: Green arrowhead-shaped leaves. White, saucer-like summer flowers. *S. latifolia* has broad leaves, *S. sagittifolia* 'Flore Pleno' (*S. japonica*) has narrow leaves, double flowers. **Hardiness:** To –20°F/–29°C. **Planting:** In moist soil or in water to 6 in. deep. Full sun or part shade.

Canna Hybrids
Description: Large, lance-shaped leaves may be rich green, bronzy red, or variegated. Showy flower spikes are red, orange, yellow, pink, cream, white, or bicolored in summer, fall. **Hardiness:** To 0°F/–18°C. **Planting:** In moist, rich soil or in water to 6 in. deep. Best in a sunny, hot spot.

Cardinal Flower
Lobelia cardinalis
Description: Single-stemmed plant with spikes of 1-in. scarlet tubular flowers in summer. **Hardiness:** To –40°F/–40°C. **Planting:** In moist soil or water to 2 in. deep. Full sun or part shade.

Cattail
Typha spp.
Description: Long, sword-like or linear leaves. Cylindrical brown flower heads in summer. Pygmy cattail (*T. minima*), 1–1½ ft. tall, is best for small ponds. **Hardiness:** Some species to –40°F/–40°C. **Planting:** In moist soil or in water to 6 in. deep for *T. minima*; 12 in. deep for larger species. Invasive; best in pots. Full sun or part shade.

Daylily
Hemerocallis hybrids
Description: Evergreen, semievergreen, and deciduous; arching, sword-shaped leaves; lily-like spring or summer flowers in a wide range of colors. Some bloom again later; others bloom throughout warm weather. **Hardiness:** To –40°F/–40°C. **Planting:** In moist, rich soil or in water to 4 in. deep. Full sun; part shade in hottest climates.

Elephant's Ear, Taro
Colocasia esculenta
Description: Succulent stalks hold huge (up to 3 ft. long) heart-shaped green leaves from spring through fall. Some forms have black or purple stalks and foliage. **Hardiness:** To 20°F/–7°C. **Planting:** In moist, rich soil or in water to 10 in. deep. Best in warm, filtered sun.

MARGINAL AND BOG PLANTS (continued)

Florida Swamp Lily, Bog Lily
Crinum americanum
Description: Intensely fragrant, spidery white flowers in 5-in. clusters from spring to fall. Clumps of strap-like green foliage. **Hardiness:** To 10°F/–12°C. **Planting:** In moist, rich soil or in water to 6 in. deep. Set tops of bulb necks even with soil surface. Full sun or part shade.

Horsetail
Equisetum spp.
Description: Rigidly upright, dark green hollow stems with horizontal dark bands. *E. hyemale* can reach 4 ft. tall; *E. scirpoides* grows only 6–8 in. **Hardiness:** To –30°F/–34°C. **Planting:** In moist soil or in water to 6 in. deep for *E. hyemale* and to 1 in. deep for *E. scirpoides*. Invasive; best in pots. Full sun or part shade.

Hosta spp.
Description: Main feature is a broad mound of overlapping leaves, which are rounded to lance-shaped, shiny or dull, smooth or textured, in shades of green, chartreuse, blue, or gray. Many selections are edged or marked with a contrasting color. Thin spikes of lavender or white trumpet-shaped flowers in summer. Makes a great backdrop for showier pond plants. **Hardiness:** To –40°F/–40°C. **Planting:** In moist, rich soil. Part or full shade.

Iris spp.
Description: Sword-like green leaves and showy flowers. Water-loving species include blue flag, *I. versicolor* (violet-blue blooms); Japanese iris, *I. ensata* (purple, violet, pink, rose, red, white); *I. laevigata* (violet, magenta, white); and yellow flag, *I. pseudacorus* (bright yellow, ivory, pale yellow). **Hardiness:** Some species to –50°F/–46°C. **Planting:** In moist, rich soil or in water to 6 in. deep (to 10 in. deep for *I. pseudacorus*). Full sun or light shade.

Ligularia spp.
Description: Large rounded or lobed leaves topped by yellow to orange daisies. Blooms in summer or into fall. **Hardiness:** To –30°F/–34°C. **Planting:** In moist, rich soil. Most thrive in part or full shade.

Lizard's Tail, American Swamp Lily
Saururus cernuus
Description: Heart-shaped deep green leaves turn crimson in fall. Tiny, fragrant, creamy white summer flowers on thin, curving spikes. **Hardiness:** To –30°F/–34°C. **Planting:** In moist soil or in water to 6 in. deep. Full sun or part shade.

Marsh Marigold
Caltha palustris

Description: Rounded, glossy green, toothed leaves 2–7 in. wide. Clusters of 2-in. bright yellow flowers in late winter, early spring. There are white-flowered and double-flowered forms. **Hardiness:** To –30°F/–34°C. **Planting:** In moist soil or in water to 6 in. deep. Full sun or part shade.

Marsh Trefoil, Bog Bean
Menyanthes trifoliata

Description: Long-stalked, three-lobed olive green leaves. Pink buds open to white or purplish star-shaped, fringed flowers in spring. **Hardiness:** To –40°F/–40°C. **Planting:** In moist soil or in water to 4 in. deep. Full sun or part shade.

Monkey Flower
Mimulus spp.

Description: Water-loving species, all with snapdragon-like flowers on sprawling or upright stems, include *M. cardinalis* (red blooms), *M. guttatus* (yellow with red throat), and *M. ringens* (violet or white). **Hardiness:** Some species to –40°F/–40°C. **Planting:** In moist soil. *M. ringens* can grow in water to 6 in. deep. Full sun or part shade.

Parrot Feather
Myriophyllum aquaticum

Description: Whorls of feathery, emerald green leaves on trailing stems to 6 ft. long; tips emerge from water. Roots provide a good spawning area for fish. Also grown as an oxygenator. **Hardiness:** To –10°F/–23°C. **Planting:** In water to 12 in. deep. Obtains nutrients from the water, so can be planted in gravel. Full sun or part shade.

Pickerel Weed, Pickerel Rush
Pontederia cordata

Description: Long-stalked, glossy green, heart-shaped leaves to 10 in. long stand well above water. Blue flower spikes from late spring to fall. **Hardiness:** To –40°F/–40°C. **Planting:** In water to 6 in. deep. Full sun or light shade.

Primrose
Primula spp.

Description: Green foliage rosettes topped by flowers in spring, early summer. Moisture lovers include species with tiered blossoms: *P. japonica* (purple with yellow eye, white, or pink); *P. prolifera* (fragrant yellow); and *P. pulverulenta* (red to red-purple). **Hardiness:** Some species to –20°F/–29°C. **Planting:** In moist, rich, acid soil. Part or full shade; can take full sun in cool-summer climates.

Ribbon Grass, Lady's Garters
Phalaris arundinacea
Description: Stripes on green, ribbon-like leaves.
Hardiness: To −30°F/−34°C. **Planting:** In moist soil or in water to 2 in. deep. Invasive. Full sun or part shade.

Rush
Juncus spp.
Description: Clumps of leaf-like, cylindrical green or gray stems with tiny flowers near stem tips. Most are grown for vertical form; corkscrew rush (*J. effusus* 'Spiralis') features twisting stems. **Hardiness:** Some species to −30°F/−34°C. **Planting:** In moist soil or in water to 4 in. deep. Full sun or part shade.

Sedge
Carex spp.
Description: Hardy, grass-like perennial with colorful leaves that provide texture year-round. Up to 2,000 species that vary in height from 6 in. to 5 ft. Color and leaf form also vary. **Hardiness:** To −20°F/−29°C. **Planting:** In moist soil or in water to 4 in. deep. Leaf color most intense in full sun.

Spike Rush
Eleocharis spp.
Description: Clumps of graceful, green, grassy stems. *E. montevidensis* grows to about 1 ft. tall. *E. dulcis* (*E. tuberosa*), to 3 ft. tall, has edible round tubers (Chinese water chestnuts) at ends of underground runners. **Hardiness:** Some species to −10°F/−23°C. **Planting:** In moist soil or in water to 2 in. deep for *E. montevidensis;* in water to 12 in. deep for *E. dulcis.* Full sun or part shade.

Sweet Flag
Acorus spp.
Description: Fans of grass-like leaves resemble miniature iris; may be entirely green or striped with cream or white. Some dwarf forms are less than 1 ft. tall.
Hardiness: Some species to −30°F/−34°C. **Planting:** In moist, rich soil or in water to 6 in. deep (to 2 in. deep for dwarfs). Full sun or part shade.

Umbrella Grass, Umbrella Palm
Cyperus spp.
Description: Umbrella-like, leafy green whorls atop triangular stems. Choices include *C. alternifolius,* to 3 ft. tall, and *C. papyrus,* a dramatic accent 6–10 ft. tall. **Hardiness:** Some species to 20°F/−7°C. **Planting:** In moist, rich soil or in water to 6 in. deep for larger species; or to 2 in. deep for smaller types. Full sun or part shade.

Variegated Manna Grass
Glyceria maxima 'Variegata'
Description: Strap-like striped leaves. **Hardiness:** To –20°F/ –29°C. **Planting:** In moist soil or in water to 6 in. deep. Full sun or part shade.

Water Canna
Thalia dealbata
Description: Long-stalked, paddle-shaped, bluish green leaves to 1½ ft. long. Foliage topped by violet-blue flower spikes to 8 in. long in summer. **Hardiness:** To –10°F/–23°C. **Planting:** In moist soil or in water to 24 in. deep. Full sun.

Water Hyssop
Bacopa monnieri
Description: Sprawling ground cover with succulent ¾-in. green leaves. Small white or pale blue flowers, spring into fall. **Hardiness:** To 10°F/–12°C. **Planting:** In moist soil at edge of slow-moving stream or pond. Will often extend shoots to float in water and send down long roots. Full sun or part shade.

Water Primrose
Ludwigia spp.
Description: Many species—some big and shrubby, others small and floating. Small, typically yellow flowers during warm weather. **Hardiness:** To 40°F/40°C. **Planting:** In moist, rich soil or in water to 6 in. deep (1 in. for smaller types). Full sun or part shade.

resource guide

The following list includes organizations, manufacturers, and retail sources that you might find helpful in creating your garden pool, fountain, or waterfall. Whenever possible, patronize suppliers in your own community and those dedicated to environmentally responsible manufacturing processes and products. To find a local supplier, check online sources listed here for dealers in your ZIP code or look in the Yellow Pages under these headings: Stone—Natural, Stone—Landscaping, Quarries, Rock, Building Materials, Masonry, Gravel and Sand, Landscape Equipment and Supplies, Pool and Pond Supplies, and Water Gardens.

Organizations and Associations

American Nursery and Landscape Association
www.anla.org
202-789-2900

American Society of Landscape Architects
www.asla.org
202-898-2444, 888-999-2752

Associated Koi Clubs of America
www.akca.org

Association of Pool & Spa Professionals
www.apsp.org
703-838-0083

Association of Professional Landscape Designers
www.apld.org
717-238-9780

Building Materials Reuse Association
www.buildingreuse.org
800-990-2672

International Water Lily & Water Gardening Society
www.iwgs.org
585-293-9144

The Masonry Advisory Council
www.maconline.org
847-297-6704
Provides information about masonry design and products

National Pond Society
800-742-4701

Materials, Stone, and Construction Products

Advanced Pavement Technology
www.advancedpavement.com
877-882-3071
Permeable paver systems

Allan Block Corporation
www.allanblock.com
952-835-5309
Stackable block for retaining walls and vertical walls

Bourget Bros.; Bourget Flagstone Co.
www.bourgetbros.com
310-450-6556
Natural stone, tile, pebbles, and custom building materials

Buechel Stone Corporation
www.buechelstone.com
800-236-4473
Quarried limestone for building and landscaping

Butterfield Color
www.butterfieldcolor.com
800-282-3388
Concrete colorant, stains, stamps

The Colonial Stoneyard
www.thecolonialstoneyard.com
978-448-3329
Natural stone and stone products for landscaping

Concrete Art
www.concreteart.net
800-500-9445
Decorative scoring and staining system

Coverall Stone, Inc.
www.coverallstone.com
800-779-3234
Natural stone columns, tiles, pebbles, fountains, benches

Cultured Stone
www.culturedstone.com
800-255-1727
Manufactured stone

EP Henry Corporation
www.ephenry.com
800-444-3679
Concrete pavers, blocks, veneers

GardenMolds
www.gardenmolds.com
800-588-7930
Steppingstone and edging molds for concrete

General Shale Brick
www.generalshale.com
800-414-4661
Brick, concrete masonry, clay, and concrete pavers, wall systems

Goshen Stone Co., Inc.
www.goshenstone.com
413-268-7171
Natural stone

High Plains Stone
www.highplainsstone.com
303-791-1862
Building, masonry, and landscaping stone

Hi-Tech Architectural Products
www.granitepaving.com
Granite and concrete cobbles and pavers

The Home Depot
www.homedepot.com
Building and landscaping materials, patio furnishings

Keystone Retaining Wall Systems
www.keystonewalls.com
800-747-8971
Retaining wall systems

Lang Stone Company
www.langstone.com
800-589-5264
Full range of natural stone products

Little Meadows Stone Co.
www.stonebtb.com/littlemeadowsstone
866-305-3250
Natural Pennsylvania landscape stone

Lowe's
www.lowes.com
Building and landscaping materials, patio furnishings

L & W Stone Corporation
www.lwstonecorp.com
800-346-9739
Natural stone pavers, boulders, veneer

Lyngso Garden Materials, Inc.
www.lyngsogarden.com
650-364-1730
Natural stone, construction materials

Manufacturer's Mineral Co.
425-228-2120
Natural rock, concrete, and masonry

Marenakos Rock Center
www.marenakos.com
425-392-3313
Full-service stone yard, specializing in natural stone for paths, walls, and water features

Modello Designs
www.modelloconcrete.com
800-663-3860
Concrete patterns and decorative finishes

Mutual Materials
www.mutualmaterials.com
800-477-3008
Manufacturer and distributor of masonry and hardscape products

Oly-Ola Edgings
www.olyola.com
800 EDGINGS
Path edging products

Original Color Chips
www.originalcolorchips.com
800-227-8479
Concrete coatings and finishes

Pacific Stone Co. Inc.
www.pacificstoneco.com
888-722-7866
Natural stone for patios, pathways, and garden walls; concrete paving stone, decorative step stones, and block retaining walls

Paver Search
www.paversearch.com
Paver products and resources

SoCal Custom Concrete
www.socalcustomconcrete.com
714-265-7134
Stamped concrete, coatings, resurfacing and other finishes

Soil Retention
www.soilretention.com
800-346-7995
Plantable and permeable concrete wall and paving systems

Sonoma Cast Stone
www.sonomastone.com
877-939-9929
Concrete tile and pavers

StoneDeck West, Inc.
www.stonedeckwest.com
877-686-4759
Natural stone decking systems

The Stone Yard
www.stoneyard.com
800-231-2200
Natural building and landscaping stone

Sure-loc Edging
www.surelocedging.com
800-787-3562
Aluminum and steel landscape and paver edging

Pool, Pond, Water Plant, and Fish Suppliers

The sources listed below can supply you with everything from flexible liners and fiberglass shells to submersible pumps and oxygenating plants. Some mail-order sources even ship goldfish and koi—by express mail, of course. This is only a partial listing, including a sampling of large, national suppliers. Smaller, regional companies, plus those specializing in water plants or fish, are widely available. Garden pool enthusiasts and builders can steer you to local favorites in your region.

Aquasculpture by Nanasi
www.aquasculpture.com
514-344-3474

Aquatic Eco-Systems Inc.
www.aquaticeco.com
877-347-4788

Flotec
www.flotecpump.com
800-365-6832

Lilypons Water Gardens
www.lilypons.com
800-999-5459

Maryland Aquatic Nurseries Inc.
www.marylandaquatic.com
877-736-1807

Moore Water Gardens
www.moorewatergardens.com
519-782-4052

Oasis Water Gardens
www.oasiswatergardens.com
206-767-9776

Paradise Water Gardens
www.paradisewatergardens.com
800-955-0161

Perry's Water Gardens
www.perryswatergarden.net
828-524-3264

Serenity Water Gardens
www.serenitywatergardens.com
678-513-6945

S. Scherer and Sons
www.waterlilyfarm.com
631-261-7432

Tetra Pond
www.tetrapond.com
800-423-6458

Van Ness Water Gardens
www.vnwg.com
800-205-2425

Waterford Gardens
www.waterford-gardens.com
201-327-0721

Water Garden Creations
www.watergardencreations.com
888-895-4465

Wicklein's Water Gardens and Native Plants
www.wickleinaquatics.com
800-382-6716

credits

Photography

John Abernathy/Photolibrary: 47 bottom; **ACP Syndication:** 148; **Thomas Alamy/GAP Photos:** 169 bottom left; **Amateur Gardening/IPC + Syndication:** 147 bottom left; courtesy of **Ames True Temper:** 84 top row #4; **Scott Atkinson:** 93 top middle; **Lee Avison/GAP Photos:** 166 top right; **Jean-Pierre Bellemare/ Jardin Botanique de Montréal:** 161 bottom center; **Mark Bolton/ Homes & Gardens/IPC + Syndication:** 147 top center; **Elke Borkowski/GAP Photos:** 52 (design: Leeds City Council), 62 top; **Paul Bousquet:** 159 bottom (design: Joe Tomocik, Denver Botanic Gardens); **Brand X Pictures/Getty Images:** 85 bottom row #4; **Marion Brenner:** 8 (design: Isabelle Greene), 10 bottom (design: Isabelle Greene), 19 top (design: Bernard Trainor + Associates), 21 (design: James David), 23 (design: Mosaic Gardens), 27 top left (design: Arcadia Studio), 27 bottom (design: Brandon Tyson), 38 top, 39 (design: Ward & Child), 48 (design: Jarrod Baumann, Zeterre), 53 bottom (design: Elliot Goliger, Artisans Landscape), 58 (design: Suzanne Biaggi Design), 63 (design: Lutsko Associates), 66 top (design: Suzanne Biaggi Design), 66 bottom right (design: Roger Warner), 73 middle (design: Andrea Cochran Land- scape Architecture), 73 right (design: Randy Thueme), 75 right, 76, 79 bottom right, 80 (design: Bernard Trainor + Associates), 87 right (design: Randy Thueme), 88 (design: Thomas Hobbes), 102 (design: Isabelle Greene), 103 both, 104 all, 105 all, 106, 107 both, 108 all, 110 left (design: John Showers), 111 all, 120 top left (design: Feyerabend and Madden Design), 130 bottom left (design: Roger Warner), 139 top center (design: Suzanne Biaggi Design), 147 bottom right (design: Bernard Trainor + Associates), 154 (design:

index

H. 1/13